God
Allows
U-Turns®

TRUE STORIES

for
women

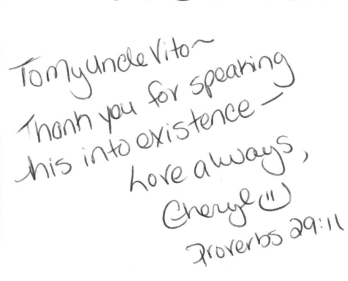

To my uncle Vito~
Thank you for speaking
this into existence—
Love always,
Cheryl ☺
Proverbs 29:11

allison bottke

and Cheryll Hutchings

God Allows U-Turns

TRUE STORIES

for women

the choices we make

change the story of our life©

BETHANY HOUSE PUBLISHERS

Minneapolis, Minnesota

Published by Bethany House Publishers
11400 Hampshire Avenue South
Bloomington, Minnesota 55438

Bethany House Publishers is a division of
Baker Publishing Group, Grand Rapids, Michigan.

Printed in the United States of America

Library of Congress Cataloging-in-Publication Data

God allows U-turns for women : the choices we make change the story of our life / [compiled by] Allison Bottke and Cheryll Hutchings.
    p. cm.
    Summary: "These affirming stories of powerful and passionate faith—perfect for devotional readings—inspire women to live their daily lives for the Lord. Real-life stories of love, forgiveness, prayer and more inspire and encourage"—Provided by publisher.
    ISBN 0-7642-0180-8 (pbk.)
    1. Christian women—Prayer-books and devotions—Engish. I. Bottke, Allison.
II. Hutchings, Cheryll.

BV4844.G63   2006
242'.643—dc22

                                        2005032498

For Kevin
I thank God that I had the good sense to choose you, because
being married to you has changed my life. I love you.

For Robert With Love
Thanks for being the one earthly constant in a life that's been
full of ups and downs. Your patience and understanding during
the development of these new books has been appreciated
more than you can know.

Table of Contents

CHAPTER **one:** **Choosing to Forgive**   **11**

The Choice of Forgiveness *by Suzannah Willingham*
The Long Miracle *by Debbye Butler*
My Favorite Color Is Red *by Tammy Gehman*
A Tidal Wave of Hope *by Jeannette Light*
For Better or Worse *by Diane H. Pitts*

CHAPTER **two:** **Choosing to Triumph**   **31**

Bold as a Lion *by Elena Chevalier*
Johnny's House *by Margaret A. Shauers*
Conquering Silence *by Carol McGalliard*
I Will Not Be Afraid *by Eva Marie Everson*
Unrecognized Blessings *by Phyllis Farringer*
Victory Over Anxiety *by Sue Foster*
Meeting Kelly *by Geri Moran*
A Test of Faith *by Susan Kelly Skitt*
Purpose of Life *by Patricia S. Toornman Bales*
Do You Want to Get Well? *by Cindy Powell*

CHAPTER **three:** **Choosing to Be a Friend**   **69**

Saving Babies *by Dianna Graveman*
A Gift of Memories *by Anne Goodrich*

Emma *by Julie Mathiason-Bendel*
Dinner With Sinners *by Tonya Ruiz*
On Wings and a Prayer *by Karen Kosman*
Walking the Walk *by Nancy B. Gibbs*
Lessons of a Lifetime *by Elaine Ingalls Hogg*

CHAPTER four: **Choosing to Pray**   **93**

Two Carloads From Peru *by Janet Carpenter*
God's Surprises *by Esther M. Bailey*
Righting a Wrong *by Connie Sturm Cameron*
A Definite Answer *by Betty Z. Walker*
The Woman Next Door *by Brenda Sprayue*

CHAPTER five: **Choosing to Take a Stand**   **113**

No One Will Know *by Jennifer Devlin*
How God Spoke to Me *by Nancy Baker*
It's All in the Timing *by Shelly Beach*
Eagle's Note *by Rita E. Billbe as told by Cheryl Taylor*
Why Now, Lord? *by Kriss Erickson*
God Used Baby Booties *by Venice Correll Kichura*

CHAPTER six: **Choosing Life**   **137**

Living the Passionate Life! *by Connie Pombo*
Dying for a Crown *by Sharon L. Fawcett*
Was Blind But Now I See *by Marie Golden Partain*
When Love Held My Hand *by Jaye Lewis*
Living in the Faith Zone *by Betty J. Johnson*
Precious Emma *by Darla Noble*

Lessons From Monterey Street *by Cheryl Haggard*
Waiting at the Crossroads *by Sharen Watson*

CHAPTER seven: **Choosing Salvation**   **173**

The Bride *by Carol Genengels*
From New Age Spirituality to the Foot of the Cross
     by Pamela V. Norton
The Lemonade Stand *by Gayle Zinda*
His Reflection *by Janet Eckles*
Single *by Maggie Normile*
The Doll in the Attic *by Marcia Krugh Leaser*
Ever After *by Carolyn Byers Ruch* as told by Christina Greene

CHAPTER eight: **Choosing Love**   **205**

I Am Woman, Hear Me Roar? *by Nancy C. Anderson*
Julia *by Kathy Pride*
Watching Over You *by Linda Ferris*
My Family's Hands *by Sharon Fink*
First You Ask *Why?* *by Pamela D. Hallal*
The Homeless Heart *by Renee Willa Hixson*
A Wreath and a Cup of Tea *by Margaret Lang*

choosing to forgive

*The Lord said to me, "Go, show your love to your wife again,
though she is loved by another and is an adulteress. Love
her as the Lord loved the Israelites, though they turn
to other gods and love the sacred raisin cakes."*

—Hosea 3:1

It is hard to imagine the story of Hosea. Told to marry an adulterous
wife and love her even after her unfaithfulness, he is an excellent
example of how much God loves us in spite of our failings and
unfaithfulness to Him. If He can forgive and draw us back, can we
not offer the same forgiveness to those around us? It is a simple
concept but hard to live out, especially if the one wronged is our
child or husband. I can forgive more easily if the wrong is done to
me, but I fight like a tigress to protect my own. God watched a
fallen world beat, torture, and crucify His only Son, and yet He for-
gives. Don't expect to be able to do the same on your own. You aren't
God. But, thankfully, He is and will help you do whatever He calls
you to do.

The Choice of Forgiveness

by Suzannah Willingham
SPARTANBURG, SOUTH CAROLINA

"Bear with each other and forgive whatever grievances you may have against one another. Forgive as the Lord forgave you" (Colossians 3:13).

"Okay, which one of us is moving out?" These words hung in the air like a knife poised to cut. How was it possible we had reached this point? From the beginning, we agreed divorce was never to be an option. Married for almost twenty years, we'd weathered all kinds of storms. Yet here was a wall so high it could not be scaled, an emotional impasse too painful to navigate.

On the surface, for the entire world to see, we were the perfect couple. We met at a Bible study and married less than a year later, knowing God meant us to be together. Even with the certainty of God's blessing on our marriage, we were unprepared for the emotional struggles to come. We never dreamed the differences in our personalities and upbringings would so greatly impact the dynamics of how we related to each other.

Shortly after our engagement picture appeared in the paper, a well-intentioned elderly woman pulled me aside at church and said, "Congratulations on your engagement, dear. I only hope you are up to the challenge. Your marriage is the hardest job you'll ever have." She squeezed my arm and smiled knowingly before walking down the hall. I stared at her retreating back in disbelief. *What a foolish old woman,* I thought. *She has no idea how much we love each other. Marriage will not be work for us!*

However, if I had been honest with myself, I would have acknowledged I felt some emotional barriers during our courtship. I passed over them lightly, giddy with love, and convinced myself they would disappear once we married. But almost immediately following the wedding, we encountered emotional issues. My husband emotionally posted a No Trespassing sign and met my efforts at discussion with a sullen stare and silence. In those early days, that was enough to make me back off from further confrontation.

Though things were not always difficult, and we went about the business of setting up a household and a life together with joy and excitement. Yet the emotional distance still remained.

As we began to try to have children, we discovered we had to travel the road of infertility. It was a tedious, stressful process—one that neither of us wanted to share with more than select friends and family. A few short weeks before our sixth anniversary, the birth of our daughter brought us joy beyond belief. For several years we were absorbed in caring for her and watching her grow until we again began the process of trying to have a child.

This time we knew what to expect. There were not as many unknowns. For me, the birth of our son completed our family. Both pregnancies were difficult to achieve and maintain, and it was a miracle we had two healthy full-term babies.

Yet my husband wanted more children. When he approached me on the subject, I was unwilling to even entertain the idea. My father had just died following a battle with cancer, and it was too overwhelming for me to think of traveling the road of a medically aided pregnancy again.

Sensing my reluctance, my husband's request came in the form

Choosing to Forgive

of a letter. To me, his chosen method of communication seemed totally impersonal and cold. I dealt with the issue by ignoring the letter. He never mentioned it again. I assumed he understood; he thought I had rejected him. Our failure to communicate on this subject added blocks to the growing wall.

There were other hurts we did not face, and we soon adopted a pattern of negativism and criticism toward each other that infected our relationship and removed honor and respect from our marriage. Tenderness and compassion were replaced by their inferior counterparts, rigidity and harshness. The process was gradual, but over time we grew so emotionally distant, being apart was preferable to being together.

So now, here we stood, with angry eyes and hostile hearts, threatening to end what had begun so long ago. Neither of us was willing to give up on our relationship, but lacking the necessary tools to affect the repairs our marriage needed, the future looked bleak.

In desperation, I turned to counseling as a means to sort through the baggage of our lives. At first my husband was resistant and angry about my desire for counseling. I made, and then canceled, an appointment before finally going alone, without my husband's knowledge.

Following my first session, I left the counselor's office with righteous smugness, having vented all my husband's ills. Mercifully, the counselor was patient, waiting several months before gently forcing me to look at my own anger and its contribution to our crumbling relationship. Each of us had stockpiled years of hurts. Having never talked our way through these hurts, we continued to use them as an arsenal of ever-ready ammunition to fuel our anger and withdrawal.

Finally able to see I was contributing to our failing marriage just as much as he was, we had a choice to make. We could forgive and move on together or go the path of so many around us and decide it was too difficult to make an about-face.

We chose to forgive. Through a slow, often painful, process, we unearthed long-buried hurts. We discussed them, sometimes only with the help of the counselor, and then extended the gift of forgiveness. It wasn't easy. Yet given the example of God's grace and mercy, how could we do less? Once our focus shifted from criticism and wounding to affirmation and forgiveness, emotional intimacy and a desire to be together gradually returned.

Last week I woke to my husband's whisper in my ear, "Happy First-Date Anniversary." I was touched he would remember a date that to others would be insignificant. As we snuggled together in the predawn hours, we thanked God for His faithfulness and for the gift of forgiveness modeled for us more than two thousand years ago. Because we made the choice to forgive, we're experiencing the excitement of taking our relationship to a level we've never known before.

Restoration of our relationship is as gradual a process as its deterioration. Some days it feels as if we take two steps forward and one back. It is easy to fall into old patterns of behavior. But with God's help, we continue to dismantle the emotional wall one block at a time and look to the future with joy, hope, and confidence.

The Long Miracle

by Debbye Butler

INDIANAPOLIS, INDIANA

I knew the story of Jesus as well as any little girl could know it. I knew my prayers—even the Lord's Prayer. My big sister taught me that. And I knew the words to "Jesus Loves Me." But I was still lost . . . to a world of seclusion, distrust, and shame. "Jesus, *do* you love me?" I wondered aloud. "Am I bad?"

When I was a tiny six-year-old girl, I became the victim of a perversion taking place regularly in my home: sexual molestation by a live-in older stepbrother. He was a teenager when he abused me, but because I was so small for my age and he was older and bigger, I thought of him as an adult. And I bought into his lies and sin. I did whatever he asked—things I would never consider, even with a marriage partner.

One day I started hiding in my bedroom closet. I stuffed myself in there like a piece of lost clothing that gets dropped in a lost-and-found box. The dark closet became my safe haven—a refuge from this unspeakable ugliness that wouldn't go away for six long years. That's a lifetime to a child.

He made my world dark and scary instead of light and playful. He made me hate my childhood. I wanted to be a "good girl," but I grew up feeling quite the opposite, even after the abuse stopped. I was bad. I was ugly. I was unlovable. I believed I deserved every horrible thing that happened to me.

And that's the ugly preface to this, the long miracle of my life.

It was in that closet God filled me with His strength so I could emotionally survive the childhood travesty haunting me and thousands of other youngsters each year. I can't explain how I knew, even as a little girl, God would get me through this never-ending nightmare. But there was no question in my mind—not then, and not now. I knew instinctively about God. If I had no other calm in my young life, I had spiritual peace.

It frightens me to think about the choices I may have made without God's abiding love and strength enveloping me. The only way I survived the trauma was with His presence. Otherwise I most surely would have become addicted to drugs or alcohol, been promiscuous or perhaps even had suicidal thoughts. I did not have the wherewithal to deliver myself from the bondage of this shame. It came from a higher power.

I have always known God did not *put* me through it, but He *got* me through it. Romans 5:3–5 could not be more applicable: ". . . We also rejoice in our sufferings, because we know that suffering produces perseverance; perseverance, character; and character, hope. And hope does not disappoint us, because God has poured out his love into our hearts by the Holy Spirit, whom he has given us."

I have always thanked Jesus for helping me to survive the silent suffering. What I failed to do all these decades was truly have a forgiving heart toward the man who shattered my childhood. Deep inside, I've wanted to forgive him for a long time, knowing it's what Jesus wants. He said in Luke 6:37, "Forgive, and you will be forgiven."

So I've spent the past few years praying for Christ to help me say—and *mean*—those healing words, "I forgive you." Part of my prayer was to ask God not to call me home until I was able to forgive the few people who have hurt me to the core of my being—the serious, life-altering sorts of hurts. I didn't want to go to my grave, much less heaven, with a speck of hate in my heart.

I hadn't communicated with my perpetrator for more than thirty-one years, but we share someone special in our lives—our sister—whose presence in my world has made an incomprehensible contribution to my faith and life. She told me for years her brother had dedicated his life to the Lord, but my bitterness would not allow me to believe it.

While visiting me in the summer of 1999 she said she had something to tell me. "He's entered counseling for his past sinful sexual behavior against you," she revealed. "And he has dedicated his life to serving Jesus."

I don't know if he had other victims; I'd always suspected it. Sex offenders usually have a lifetime pattern. And I don't know what made him decide to seek counseling. But knowing he finally admitted what he had done made all the difference. It was all I needed to know—that he had confessed this sin, not to me, but to others—most especially to Jesus, the Great Healer.

The next words out of my mouth came as unexpectedly to me as they did to my sister. Teary-eyed and with a cracked voice, I said, "Tell him I forgive him." I *meant* it.

She left the room momentarily. I suspect it was to do exactly what I was doing: crying, regaining composure, and telling God, "Thank you for this healing moment." She delivered my message weeks later, to which her brother replied, "Tell her I'm sorry for any pain I caused her."

When I look back on my life, I remember how I got stuffed in a lost-and-found box. You could have one, too. It might be a street corner, a courtroom, a jail cell, a hospital bed, or a church pew on a Decision Sunday. For me, it was a bedroom closet. I was quietly united with Christ, who began preparing me to walk in His way and do His work, equipping me with His abundant strength for survival, and walking side-by-side with me on a journey toward forgiveness, which took decades.

Nearly two years after our conversation, my sister and I were together for another life-changing event. Our dad lay dying, and the entire family was summoned to his bedside. It meant I would be face-to-face with my stepbrother for the first time in thirty-three years. He approached me in the nursing-home hallway.

"Debbye, can I talk to you a minute?" he asked gently. "I want to tell you I'm sorry for what I did and ask you to forgive me."

"I do," I replied. "It's in the past."

We both were healed, and the burden of sin miraculously lifted from our shoulders. Once more, my Lord wiped my tears, held my hand, and showed me the way. He took my heart of stone and gave me a new one, as He had promised.

Through the power of our Lord and Savior, I am a little girl lost . . . and found.

My Favorite Color Is Red

by Tammy Gehman
ALLENTOWN, PENNSYLVANIA

I can't believe I'm here. Just the thought of walking through the front door of my church created a sickening twist in my stomach. "Settle down, Tam—you're okay," I whispered to myself.

But I was not okay. My life was in shambles.

How could Kevin do this to me . . . to us? I trusted him.

What's more, beyond that solid steel door sat several women just like me. Their husbands were sex addicts, too.

Someone is bound to recognize me. What am I going to do? But then again, could the strangulating roots of shame cause any more damage?

My trembling hands reached for the door handle. I entered the room and anxiously scanned to see who was there. The chairs, arranged in a circle formation, made it difficult to see the faces of the individuals.

I repositioned myself to take a closer look. At that time, a pair of espresso-brown eyes connected with mine. *Oh God, not Joanne's marriage, too.* No words were exchanged, but at that moment, we heard each other. We understood the emptiness in our tear-filled eyes. We recognized each other's heartache. We were acquainted with the fear, the humiliation, the anger, and the mistrust that was within us.

Barbara, the head of the counseling department, interrupted our gaze. "Hi, Tammy," she said, "come sit down." She pointed to the only empty chair in the circle . . . it was next to Joanne.

"What each of you has done tonight took a lot of courage."

Barbara paused as she looked each one of us in the eyes. "You've made a huge step to begin your journey toward healing, and I'm proud of you."

She placed her hand on the woman's shoulder sitting next to her. "I want to introduce you to Sonya. She has walked your current path, and because of that, she will be facilitating this group."

Are you crazy? I thought as I looked at this beautiful woman in her mid-fifties. *If I were you, I'd never want to talk about this subject matter again—let alone facilitate a group!*

For the next twenty minutes, Sonya shared her story. She disclosed how pornographic movies, nude beaches, and multiple affairs invaded her marriage.

"The night he threatened my life," she continued, "was the last time I saw him."

She leaned forward in her chair. "Girls," she said in a soft but firm voice, "this addiction has *nothing* to do with you."

I could no longer keep it together. "Oh God," I cried, "if this has nothing to do with me, then how come I feel like a failure?"

For the remainder of the evening, Sonya encouraged us to share our stories. She heard cries from those who found pornographic materials in their homes, strip club receipts in their husband's pockets, or outrageous telephone bills in the mail. She listened as some had checked the history on their computers only to set their eyes on pornographic images that are now permanently etched in their minds. She empathized with one who was devastated by the loss of the full-time ministry she had shared with her husband.

Finally, after all of these years of silence, I have found a place to speak.

With each meeting, the bond between our group grew tighter. We cheered, we cried, we hugged, we prayed, we encouraged— whatever the emotion—we experienced it. Together.

Little did I know months later I would attend a meeting that would change my life.

"Tonight we're going to begin this meeting a little differently," Sonya smiled. "I want to give you an opportunity to talk and share what is on your heart." It was as if she read my mind.

"I'm mad!" I blurted out in disgust.

Sonya remained silent as if she knew I needed to keep talking.

"I'm mad that *my* life has been turned upside down because of *his* addiction. I'm mad at him for the choices he's made. I'm mad that I can't trust him. I'm mad at the way I reacted last week when . . ." my voice trailed off.

"Go on," she said as she leaned in toward me.

"Last Friday Kevin called and said he'd be home by four o'clock. He was late. At 4:05 I was in the bathroom vomiting. I heard him throw his keys in the key basket at 4:07," I sat back in the chair. "Sonya, the man was only seven minutes late and *boom*—I'm in the bathroom throwing up."

Sonya gently moved closer to me and placed her hand in mine. "Tammy," she said with her soft voice, "as much as Kevin is addicted to pornography, *you* are addicted to Kevin."

I slumped in my chair as those words penetrated the innermost part of my being. No one spoke for what seemed like an eternity.

"Oh my word . . . you're right. I don't know who I am anymore," I said as I tried to process what she'd said. "His addiction *has* consumed my life." I looked around at my friends. "Joanne, if you were to ask me what my favorite color is, I would have no clue. If you were to ask me, Patty, what my favorite food is, I could not tell you. Emily, if you were to even ask me what I like to do on a warm summer's evening, I wouldn't know."

I left that meeting determined to make a U-turn. I shifted my dependency off of a sinful man and onto a sinless God. I spent my days falling in love again with the ultimate Bridegroom. I shared my dreams and desires with Him—the incredible Dream-giver. And my life has never been the same.

In September of 2000, I reached for the handle of my church door with confidence. I was a healed woman and the new director of the very ministry I once feared. It has been a tremendous honor for me to assist in rescuing women who are drowning in the cesspool of their husbands' sexual addiction and pornography.

And if that isn't enough . . . the healing that God has done in my marriage is beyond my comprehension. On January 9, 2001, our two boys, Ty and Tait, witnessed their mom and dad renewing their wedding vows. Our Father never ceases to amaze me.

Incidentally, I now know my favorite color is red. My favorite food is seafood. And what I like to do on a warm summer's evening is to sit next to Kevin in Camden Yards, watching the Baltimore Orioles beat their opponent. *To God be the glory—Great things He has done.*

A Tidal Wave of Hope

by Jeannette Light
TILLSON, NEW YORK

I stood in the crowded airport waiting area, stunned by the television images of ravaged towns buried under a foot of mud. The devastating news type scrolled along the bottom of the screen, reporting thousands of lives swept away by the huge tsunami. The pictures that flashed mimicked my inner turmoil. Like those on the news, I too was shocked by loss.

While this incredible tsunami rolled over a continent's shoreline, leaving devastation in its wake, another kind of tidal wave raged in my own life. After twenty-seven years of struggling in marriage and waiting for a miracle, my marriage was soon to be wiped out, taking its place as another statistic in divorced couples.

At best, my husband and I stood at the brink of legal separation. After years of enduring his Dr. Jekyll/Mr. Hyde personality, I could no longer ride the roller coaster of his emotions.

I agonized over this decision. I wanted to do God's will, but our marriage was no longer healthy for either one of us. After I returned home from Christmas vacation with our children, I planned to contact a lawyer. But the separation was beyond my understanding, since I had given my all to make our marriage work.

Amidst this turbulence, I looked forward to spending time with my children in sunny Florida, a brief respite to the start of a heart-rending process of legal separation. As thousands bereaved the death of loved ones by the devastating tsunami, I grieved for my dying marriage. And even though I felt reconciliation wouldn't be possible at this point, I still prayed for God's will, hoping for a miracle.

Returning home on New Year's Eve, I received an icy reception. Waves of despair engulfed me. The next day I had no choice but to ask my husband to leave. He refused.

"I'm calling a lawyer," I threatened.

"Go ahead, but you'll have to drag me out of here," he retaliated and stormed out of the house, giving me opportunity to pick up the phone and actually call my lawyer.

But as I pressed the keys, I found myself dialing the number of a close friend instead. "I don't understand. Why? Why hasn't God given me a miracle after I've prayed for so many years?" Confusion and deep sorrow invaded my being as I poured my heart out to her.

Later that evening my husband returned home to his own icy reception. I suspected he would follow the same old pattern, and as always, he apologized. But I wasn't going to fall for it this time.

"It's just a bunch of empty promises." I folded my arms and stood defiant. "They've become meaningless. You need to *show me* change, not just *tell* me."

He pleaded with me, "This time I'll try—really, I will."

I knew his game, his tactics. He would be nice for a few days, then become moody and sulk or insult me and lose his temper. His last outburst cost him six weeks' suspension from his job. I wouldn't fall for his lies any longer.

Again, he looked imploringly at me, yet I turned away. It hurt deeply, but I needed to be firm. I hoped creating a crisis would wake him up to his destructive habits. Perhaps then he would turn his life around. "You need to leave—now." I stood in resolve.

The following week was heartrending. I felt shipwrecked, with

Choosing to Forgive

no way out. I cried out to God, "Please, guide us through this storm." I knew my husband wanted to change, but he had lost sight of the correct course.

After a few days he came home.

"I'm going to change this time. Please, give me another chance." I wanted to believe his pleas, but I had already given him hundreds of second chances. Now he was even more persistent than usual. "I need you. I can't live without you. I'll do what I must." I was leery, yet he appeared genuine. *Could he possibly have seen the light and changed direction?* Though my mind was set, I'd allow God to alter it—if only I had some tangible evidence first.

I prayed and sensed God wanted me to ride out this storm and try again, so I came up with a plan. I made a list of five things my husband needed to do: see a psychiatrist, visit a therapist and a Christian counselor, read the Bible, and pray. He agreed to each of them. If he could follow through, then I knew rescue was possible. I scheduled an appointment for myself with a Christian counselor, while he pursued the conditions I required. Little by little I saw progress, and the waves began to subside. God had sent us a life raft, and my husband and I scrambled aboard.

After a couple of months, we attended Christian marriage counseling. In the beginning, it was painful; he was angry with me, but the counselor helped my husband untangle the knots of his anger and poor attitudes. I faced some areas in my own life that also required change.

God's hand reached into our ocean of turmoil and lifted us up. We were no longer drowning. Though we still hadn't arrived safely to shore, at least we had something to hang on to.

Then, just when our marriage was improving, another big wave hit. On a freezing cold winter day, my husband slipped on black ice and broke his ankle. He spent six weeks recovering on the couch, unable to work or do anything else. He began to sink into depression, and sometimes I felt like jumping ship, but the threat of icy cold water and God's presence kept me rowing toward land. God also extended His arms to my husband, and he climbed back onto our little raft.

But as soon as he stood, another tidal wave hit. He faced several deaths in his family, knocking him overboard again. These were close relatives he loved deeply; one was like his own father. He was miserable, almost giving up. I thought I'd lost him in the undertow of his own tsunami.

I wondered how much longer we could cling to the edge of our deflating raft. The winter dragged on, one of the worst we've ever experienced. Progress drained from my husband, as he slipped in and out of depression. I questioned my decision to stay with him, but I held to God and His promise that He would never leave me or forsake me.

Forgiving my husband was long and difficult, so I prayed for perseverance, focusing on my responsibilities while trusting God to act. Thankfully, my husband's ankle healed and the springtime came in full bloom. My husband showed signs of life, and I regained hope, just like the tsunami victims who picked up the pieces of their lives and started rebuilding.

Slowly our marriage made a U-turn and approached a safe harbor. Christ's love guided us safely back to solid ground. There were many issues to work through, but both of us learned how to deal with our difficulties more effectively. My husband gained insight into the shadows of life he had been hiding from, and I learned more about *agape* or unconditional love.

In the final aftermath of our tidal wave, God reassured us that hope floats, even on stormy waters. Our reconciled marriage is living proof of it.

For Better or Worse

by Diane H. Pitts
WILMER, ALABAMA

I couldn't walk. The knee that was working on Thursday couldn't report for duty on Saturday—even for a crawl. Although I've had arthritis for a long time, it's never been so bad I couldn't limp along. But now, no crawling, no limping, and especially no walking.

My husband, Darrell, stared at my grapefruit-sized knee. "What are you going to do?" he questioned.

I considered my options. "Well, I'm going to rest it, ice it, use crutches, and increase my medicine." As a physical therapist, I had a general idea of what would get me to first base and maybe back to work on Tuesday.

Darrell pointed to the couch. "Just sit down and I'll take care of things around here." His statement didn't surprise me; in the past three years my husband had taken on quite a few responsibilities in our household: paying bills, shopping, child care. I knew I could count on him and breathed a sigh of relief. There was, however, a time in our marriage when that type of partnership was nonexistent.

Over the years we had our share of ups and downs, fluctuating income when we had our own construction business, poor communication leading to simmering strife, and rambunctious boys enlarging our family. Problems mounted. The fairy-tale marriage slowly disintegrated into broken dreams. It was too easy to lay the problem at the other one's door.

One day while washing dishes, I listened to a cassette tape that

Choosing to Forgive

gently pointed out some of the areas I had ignored in my own life. I scrubbed dishes until they squeaked, and I glared at the tape recorder.

"I have a right to feel this way," I argued.

The speaker's next words rocked my soul: "Hold on to grudges or be changed."

She was talking to me! I had a choice to make. I began to pray.

"God, would you change me? Change *my* heart even if Darrell stays the same."

Later, through tears, I watched our wedding video and listened to the vows we had made, until death do you part, for better or worse. The look between us spoke joy. Oh, to have that tenderness again, to tap the river I knew was deep within me and I hoped was still in the man I married!

Over the next few months, the iceberg in my heart thawed. Miraculously, without saying a word, I saw God soften my husband, as well. We started the repair work to forge a more realistic marriage; deep down neither of us wanted to quit. I knew a new level had been reached when he started planning an anniversary trip to Seattle. The old barriers slowly crumbled as a new, finer marriage arose.

So here I sat on the couch, thinking about how fortunate I was to have someone to count on at a time like this. It was definitely a bad time, but maybe not the worst. I couldn't help but think of our wedding again. During those vows, Darrell and I had no idea of the ups and downs we would face. Now we knew we could weather them, the best and the worst, one choice at a time.

CHAPTER two

choosing to triumph

I can do everything though him who gives me strength. —Philippians 4:13

Rarely do we get the fairy tale. Life has so many curves, it's all we can do just to hang on. The unplanned pregnancy, the surprise lay-off, the teen who is nothing like the sweet child who once obeyed you, the husband whose memory doesn't include his marriage vows, and the body that revolts and fights health—none of which are planned and all of which can leave you feeling drained and defeated. But praise be to God, all of this and more are but a blip on His radar. He can handle it. For when we are weakest, He is the strongest. When we stand still on His promises, we can watch His power, grace, and mercy at work. We are more than conquerors in Him who created the universe and all that is in it. So stand on His promise, put on that armor, my sister, and shout out with me, "Go God!"

Bold as a Lion

by Elena Chevalier

BENTON, NEW HAMPSHIRE

"This is crazy!" I muttered to myself, watching my supervisor settle herself in the back of my first-grade classroom. "She'll only observe me for a *few minutes,* and then she'll leave." I rubbed the back of my neck, trying to convince myself to remain calm. Twenty pairs of innocent eyes stared at me, and I tried to focus on them like this was any other day.

I knew my supervisor would be coming in for a routine observation, and she knew I had a debilitating fear of people watching me, but that didn't calm the fear threatening to suffocate my confidence.

"Class, p-p-p-please finish tracing the A's. Th-th-then you may color the p-p-picture," I stammered. My hands trembled and tears filled my eyes, then spilled over. Without warning, fear overwhelmed me and I bolted from the room.

My supervisor found me sobbing in the bathroom. "You're a good teacher, Elena." Mrs. Tedder placed her hand on my shoulder and tried to soothe my anxieties. Her words seemed absurd to me. Hadn't I just run out of a classroom full of six-year-olds? "Now, pull yourself together and go back to your students. I'll speak to you after school." She left me to freshen up and get back to my job.

Back in my room, I relieved the aide who was watching my class, and the rest of the day crept by slowly. This was my first year teaching, and I was a nervous wreck. As long as it was just students in the room, I was fine. But whenever there was an adult present, I panicked. I knew I was fearful of people watching me, but I never thought I'd abandon my classroom. How could I face my supervisor now?

"Elena, you've got to conquer this fear." Mrs. Tedder had every right to reprimand me. "Go ahead and cry if you must, but stay in your room! I'll be back to observe you later this week."

Her words struck terror in my heart, but I had a choice to make. Either I would allow fear to rule my life, or I would allow God to give me the grace to deal with this.

At home that evening, I looked up Scripture verses dealing with fear. Jeremiah 1:8 (KJV) fit perfectly. "Be not afraid of their faces: for I am with thee to deliver thee, saith the Lord." How encouraging it was to know that one of God's prophets had the same problem I had.

Then I found another verse. Proverbs 28:1 (KJV) said, "The wicked flee when no man pursueth; but the righteous are bold as a lion."

Tears filled my eyes. "Lord," I prayed, "forgive me for my fear. Forgive me for running out of my classroom and not relying on you for strength. Please help me to conquer this fear of people watching me."

The following day I taped a copy of Proverbs 28:1 on my desk at school. Each time I read it, I asked God to make me "bold as a lion."

True to her word, my supervisor once again slipped into my classroom. I felt my breathing begin coming in shorter and shorter gasps. "Lord, please take my fear away," I pleaded. But the tears came anyway, flowing uncontrollably. Everything in me wanted to run again, but Scripture kept running through my mind, giving me strength. By God's grace I managed to stay put, and I breathed a sigh of relief when Mrs. Tedder left the room. I glimpsed a smile as she closed the door behind her.

Eventually I was accustomed to occasional visits from my supervisor. Inwardly I was still terrified, but outwardly a facade of calm covered my terror.

Then one day the school principal brought me more terrifying news: "Miss Belletete, three teachers from another school will be observing in your classroom today."

Panic threatened to overtake me again, but just as swiftly, the words, *Be not afraid of their faces: for I am with thee,* echoed in my mind.

When the teachers stepped into my classroom, I kept my eyes on the children, struggling to keep my voice from quivering as we recited letter blends together. I thought for certain that everyone could hear my heart; it was pounding violently. But the sound of Scripture quickly replaced my anxious heart, and I began reciting the verses in my mind. By the time the three teachers left, I felt like I'd just finished a marathon, but I was proud that I'd managed to stay in the classroom. And I didn't even cry.

Later, one of the visiting teachers complimented me on my teaching. "And you were so calm," she added. Inwardly, I laughed in amazement.

I got married that summer vacation, yet even that special day didn't erase my fear of others watching me. I trembled throughout my own ceremony. And when I returned to school in the fall, there were more challenges awaiting me.

"Mrs. Chevalier, a principal from a school in New Hampshire would like us to send someone from our phonics program. I'd like you to go." I was stunned. My principal was asking me to speak in front of adults? Not long after that, he called on me again to present a workshop at our state's Christian School Teachers Conference.

Each time I was asked to speak, I agonized for hours and days over the impossible task, but God was faithful, giving me the courage and confidence I needed. Little did I know, the preparation was being laid for experiences awaiting me in the very near future.

One night a phone call came from Mr. Straperro, the father of one of my students. "My daughter really enjoys your teaching," he explained. "She especially likes your Bible stories and your puppet skits. In fact, I've watched you do the chapel program in school, and you'd be great doing a children's program on cable TV."

I was dumbfounded; my jaw dropped open.

"We have an opening on Wednesday nights for a live show," he continued. "Are you interested?"

I just chuckled to myself. Me? The one who ran terrified out of her classroom, do a weekly TV program? Absurd. When I asked the Lord to take away my fear of people watching me, I never imagined He'd go to such lengths to answer my prayer.

Now I had a choice to make. Would I choose God's way, or mine? What was more important to me—my comfort or God's will? Did I really want to let fear keep a foothold in my life? It was an incredibly hard decision.

Less than a month later I stood in a TV studio with a blue puppet stage as a backdrop. The red light flashed On the Air.

"Hi, boys and girls! I'm Aunt Elena."

When the On the Air sign clicked off at the end of my first broadcast, my heart was beating wildly and my hands were quaking. I can't say that I wasn't afraid, but in making the choice to stand on God's Word and not to run from the things I feared, God gave me the strength to overcome my fears. And because of my choices, I found joy in trusting God and His leading. I'm truly glad I chose His way. It's true: the choices we make really do change the story of our life!

Johnny's House

by Margaret A. Shauers
GREAT BEND, KANSAS

It seems a long time ago since I started teaching my first church school class, where I met Johnny. Today I count my experience with him as one of my richest. Johnny's behavior caused my predecessor to stop teaching the class in the middle of the year. Johnny's behavior was also the reason I often wondered if I should follow her example.

Johnny ran into the street when we went for a hike. He pushed other children, pulled girls' hair, yelled, screamed, and even occasionally bit. Many of the words that came from Johnny's mouth were far from appropriate for a church school classroom. Johnny was a four-year-old handful.

The one thing Johnny liked to do was build. Once I learned this, our building blocks got quite a workout. While building, Johnny actually quit yelling. Sometimes, if the other children let him be the boss, Johnny allowed them to help him. There was only one remaining problem: Once Johnny began to build, he did not want to stop.

"Won't put up the blocks!" he would insist sullenly when I announced it was time to put the toys away and move to the worship center. That simple phrase brought us back to the yelling, screaming, and cursing.

I never did solve the problem of Johnny through any wisdom of my own. The only contributions I can claim is prayer and the ability to make fast decisions. With Johnny around I found many opportunities to pray—and these prayers were answered through Johnny.

One week I decided to pick up the blocks for Johnny. We were wasting too much time arguing.

"No, teacher, no!" Johnny screamed, grabbing the end of the first block I picked up from the large "house" outline he had strung across the floor. "Johnny just built his house. No, teacher, no!" he cried.

Then sullenly, Johnny added, "Johnny will stay in his house. Johnny will hear the story from here."

Without consciously thinking, I put the block back in place. "Very well," I said, "if you can't come with us to the worship center, we will come to you." And we all went to "Johnny's house."

Johnny's face was a mirror of surprise, doubt, and a bit of the selfishness he always showed over the blocks. But there was a fourth emotion, too. There was pride of ownership, and it won! Solemnly Johnny showed the other children where the door of his house was. Being Johnny, he was not lenient with those who tried to walk over a wall. For the first time since I started teaching the class, however, Johnny wasn't pouting or causing trouble.

Having our story in Johnny's house became routine. Because he wanted to have the most impressive house possible, Johnny began to grow lenient toward the other builders. Instead of announcing, "Johnny's going to build a house," he began to urge, "Hurry, let's build the house for our story." As he learned working together was fun, Johnny began to participate more freely and peacefully in other activities.

This change was gradual. There were still many Sundays when I wondered why I had taken the class. But the magic of Johnny's house never failed to make him happy. Each Sunday I watched him as he listened to the Bible story, and I knew I would not resign from teaching this class.

As I said, those early church school lessons often seem long past, but recently I saw them again. Johnny, now a long-legged teenager and the office helper of the day, popped into my classroom just as story time drew near.

He glanced curiously as the children, scurrying to put up cars and dolls. Then his eyes fell on several long lines of blocks, placed end to end to form the outline of a house.

"The house!" he exclaimed. "You still use it."

"Of course we still use it," I said, warmed by the glowing smile on his face. "It's the best idea anyone in this classroom has ever had." I laughed and added, "I'm glad to see you here. Now maybe I can explain why, although we have no one by that name, I still tell the children it's time to have our story in Johnny's house."

His face glowed even more brightly with pleasure, and I couldn't help compare this friendly young man to the sullen, angry four-year-old I had first known.

I should have visited in Johnny's home in the days when he was a four-year-old. If I had, I would have learned Johnny received little or no attention there. He had an infant sister and an ailing mother. There wasn't much time left for Johnny. The only thing I did have enough sense to do back then was to choose to ask for God's help. Only His help made me make the right choice one Sunday morning, a choice giving Johnny the sense of importance he so desperately needed.

Choosing to Triumph

Conquering Silence

by Carol McGalliard
GREENSBORO, NORTH CAROLINA

I didn't want to cry. I wanted to stand before Dan Allender and tell him what a wonderful job he had done in presenting the Cry of the Soul seminar. There were many similarities in our stories. I wanted to tell him how he had encouraged me with his story of overcoming childhood abuse. I wanted to tell him without crying.

"I will not cry. I will not cry. I will not cry," I said over and over again. Then I prayed, "Lord, help me not to cry. How can I ever witness to others if I cry every time I try to tell them how you are helping me overcome abuse? Please don't let me be a blubbering fool."

There was no reason to cry on this afternoon, was there? No one had broken my toys. No one yelled at me. No one made fun of my hair or my clothes. No one abused me that day. No one had beat me, then denied me the right to cry.

But I was still responding to these circumstances as I stood before Dan. I was still trying to hide my hurt, my sense of shame, the feeling that I was flawed because I was abused as a child. I wanted Dan to believe I had resolved my abuse issues and matured to emotional and spiritual adulthood. I wanted to be a Super Christian in his eyes. I wanted to be able to stand before hundreds of people as he has and say to them, "I wouldn't change what God brought to my life." I wanted to be able to do it without bursting into tears. Who would want to listen to me sniffle through my story?

"You are a walking testimony to the fact that there is a God who loves us and can fix us," I said as Dan embraced me. I told him about the book I hoped to write and promised to send him a copy.

"Whether you send me a copy or not, just tell your stories," he replied.

I began crying and stammered through my tears, "How long does it take before you stop crying when trying to tell the stories?"

He looked directly in my eyes, pointed his finger at me, and said, "I hope you never stop crying." I walked away stunned. Permission to cry even after you've forgiven? Permission to cry forever? Permission to cry!

I thought, "If it's okay to cry, what's the problem? What keeps me from giving my testimony?" Revelation 12:11 gave me the answer: "They overcame by the blood of the lamb and by the word of their testimony; they did not love their lives so much as to shrink from death." Pride. I loved my image more than I loved testifying for God.

How humbling this realization was, but also very liberating. While Satan kept me blind to my sin, he was able to keep me enslaved to him; he kept me from testifying of God's love. But with the blinders removed, I was free from his power. I now choose to stand and tell my story, praising God as I wipe away tears.

No more silence for me.

I Will Not Be Afraid

by Eva Marie Everson
CASSELBERRY, FLORIDA

I was six years old on November 22, 1963. With scant memory of the day itself, I assume I was in my first-grade classroom, unaware that half a country away, the thirty-fifth president of the United States was being assassinated in a crime that would rock the country—indeed, the world—and would bring rise to one of the most popular unanswered questions of the twentieth century: Who shot JFK?

I didn't hear of Martin Luther King's April 4, 1968, assassination until the following day. My parents spoke in hushed tones about "what the world was coming to." I was ten years old, in the sixth grade, and word was our school would begin integrating the following year. Most of our parents expressed concern about "what would happen to the children . . . the children . . ." But the children were pretty okay with it.

Two months later we were shocked by the news of presidential candidate Robert F. Kennedy's assassination. Now almost eleven years old, I too began to wonder what the world was coming to. It wasn't bad enough we had to watch a bloody war being fought every evening on the nightly news—during or just after our family dinner, no less. Our leaders were being killed.

In the last month of the seventh grade, at the age of twelve, I was assigned a final report for English. I chose the most recent newsworthy piece of turbulence to research and write about, thinking I might find some understanding as to why four young college students had been killed on the grounds of Ohio's Kent State University. My report raised more questions than it gave answers, but I can tell you even to this day, the student rioting began with discontent concerning the invasion of Cambodia and ended with the deaths of Allison Krause, Jeffrey Miller, William Schroeder, and Sandra Scheuer.

For some reason, I was beginning to take it personally.

I was about to celebrate my twentieth birthday in August 1977. I lived across the state from my childhood home and family, alone in my own apartment, and worked for the county police department. One scorching afternoon after work, I curled up on my old but comfortable sofa, reached for the nearby telephone, and placed a woman-to-woman call to my mother. As we chatted, I heard my seventeen-year-old brother's muffled voice as he spoke to our mother.

"You're kidding," my mother responded.

"What?" I asked. "What happened?"

"Van just walked in and said that Elvis died."

"Presley?" I asked, as though there could be more than one Elvis. And of course it was Elvis Presley, the king of rock 'n' roll, the man who had entertained me for as long as I could remember with his movies and rockabilly songs, and had made me swoon with his love ballads.

Almost a decade later, on a cold January day, I rushed from the grocery store where I'd been shopping. If I hurried, I could make it home in time to watch the lift-off of the space shuttle Challenger, which would be taking an ordinary citizen—a schoolteacher—into orbit for the first time. I ran into the house and turned the television on. Without breaking my stare at the screen, I stepped over to the sofa and sat down, bringing my hands up to my lips in some sort of silent prayer.

"Oh, dear God . . . dear God . . ."

The giant shuttle, engulfed in billows of smoke, lifted from the earth, spearing toward the open sky. I held my breath and bit my bottom lip. Suddenly I gasped.

"It's going to explode," I said to no one. And in that very moment, it did.

On September 11, 2001, I was in a hotel in New York City watching *Good Morning America* while my husband showered in the adjoining bathroom. Charlie Gibson was interviewing Sarah Ferguson. It was so cool to think they were a few blocks away in Times Square . . . a place we had been just the night before.

Suddenly the picture went fuzzy, an interruption in the transmission of the programming. I was agitated. But the interruption lasted only a second. The next interruption—the one that came less than thirty seconds later—lasted much longer, and I sometimes think it has wedged itself into my life and has yet to let go.

All through Manhattan, the sound of sirens filled the city streets. I grabbed my cell phone. I would attempt, for the next five hours, to reach family and friends. Sometimes we were successful, most times we weren't. I knew our children and my parents would be frantic. I wasn't prepared, however, for the outpouring of love . . . and fear . . . I heard in the voice mail of my phone when we finally gained access to the outside world.

For five days following the September 11 attacks, Dennis and I walked between the imposing skyscrapers of a city locked in. We went into two of the churches on Fifth Avenue—once spilling over with traffic, now nearly deserted—to pray . . . to search for answers that didn't seem to exist . . . to ask God for direction.

My husband and I stood outside a television studio with hundreds of others. We all stared through the high-rise glass at the monitors that kept citizens updated . . . minute by minute . . . second by second . . . and continuously replayed the scenes of two jet airplanes, screaming into explosions within the colossal structures once known as the Twin Towers of the World Trade Center.

We live just outside the city of Orlando. Shortly after our return home—shortly after our country had gone to war—I was scheduled to speak at a church downtown. As I neared the city from the interstate and saw the rise of the city skyline, my heart began to quicken. By the time my car was driving between the buildings, I had begun to panic. Twice I pulled over and attempted to compose myself. Why was this happening? I'm a strong person, not at all the kind of woman who gives in to emotional weaknesses. Still, weeks after the attacks, when I had been invited for lunch at a downtown restaurant, when the panic rose inside me again, I knew I was bearing an unseen scar on my heart.

It's not uncommon for me to see a plane as it descends toward the international airport on the south side of central Florida. I never gave it much thought before, that appearance of suspension and power. I do now.

Yesterday as I was watching television, the reception went out for a moment. Just a moment and I gasped. Had something else happened? When I knew for certain it had been nothing, I laughed, but it wasn't out of humor.

"Oh, Lord," I prayed, "show me your healing. Not just for the incidents of 9/11, but for that part of me who still cries when I walk through museums dedicated to John Fitzgerald Kennedy, that still holds on to my Vietnam POW bracelet, that still rises up in anger when I hear social injustice and statements made by ridiculous prejudices. Help me understand why people are willing to kill one another for having a difference of opinion or political views that don't see eye-to-eye. Why sometimes innocents pay for the guilty, and fame and fortune isn't always what it seems to be."

Today I sit with my Bible stretched out before me. I'm speaking at a church tonight, an event planned many months ago. They asked if I would speak on one of the Psalms. I said I would. "Psalm 46," I told them. "Be still, and know that I am God."

As I review the words of the text, as I think about what I will say before the crowd who has come to hear me speak, my eyes rest on the beginning of the song. "God is our refuge and strength, an ever-present help in trouble. Therefore we will not fear, though the earth give way and the mountains fall into the heart of the sea . . ."

I continue to read, rejoice, and soar with the jubilation at the promises held on the pages before me. "The Lord Almighty is with us; the God of Jacob is our fortress."

Our fortress. Our safe place. Perhaps not from earthly death, for many godly men and women have died in national tragedies. But from fear. Fear from assassins' bullets, from violent uprisings, from science gone amok, and from the unknown that looms just over the horizon.

"Nations are in uproar, kingdoms fall; he lifts his voice, the earth melts."

Yes, it melts, as does my fear. I will not be afraid. I will not. I will be still, and know that He is God. It's a choice I can make.

Unrecognized Blessings

by Phyllis Farringer

OLATHE, KANSAS

"When you pray for rain, be sure to carry an umbrella—and don't complain about the mud." It's a well-worn cliché reminding us God will answer our prayers—but sometimes we get more than we are expecting.

I was at a point in my Christian walk when, though my faith was growing, I knew I lacked something. I longed to know God better. I began to pray the Lord would draw me closer to Him, and teach me what it meant to truly love Him with all my heart. I think when I began to pray for greater intimacy with God, I expected to experience things like a richer prayer life and a greater understanding of Scripture. I looked for more meaningful times of worship.

But instead of experiencing those things, my life hit a sudden downward spiral: I broke my wrist, my husband and I experienced financial hardship, and I lost a valuable friendship. As pain stacked upon pain during a time I was seeking a deeper friendship with God, I wondered, "Are you listening, Lord? Is this how you treat your friends?"

I heard only silence.

Meanwhile, discomfort, inconvenience, and heartache were consuming my attention.

My wrist, shattered in a fall, needed to be set surgically. Since I would be going under a general anesthetic, the emergency room doctor could not give me anything to relieve my pain. I kept getting bumped down the surgery schedule as emergency after emergency took precedence over a broken wrist. The doctors continued withholding pain medication because they still expected to take me into surgery at any time.

With hours to do nothing but lie still and think, I eventually began to think about the pain in Jesus' wrists when He was on the cross. I knew there were verses in the Bible telling us that because Jesus suffered, He is able to understand our suffering. To look at it from another point of view, when we suffer, we get a glimpse of what He suffered, willingly, on our behalf.

The wrist accident occurred while my husband and I were in the struggling stages of building a business. Our income was practically nonexistent, and by this time our savings were depleted. Since we carried a high deductible on our insurance, we acquired a lot of medical bills at a time when our finances were already stretched to the limit. I learned more about poverty than I had ever expected to. But I also learned God provided. I remembered the verses speaking of Christ having no place to lay His head when He walked on the earth.

The broken friendship in the midst of an already difficult situation was the hardest for me to accept. Long after my wrist healed and our financial situation improved, I still ached from the pain of rejection and betrayal. Then I remembered how a friend betrayed Jesus and how all of the disciples deserted Him at the cross.

It took me a while to get it, but finally I began to see what was happening. All of the things I saw as potholes on my journey were actually signposts pointing me to the deeper relationship I longed for with the Lord. The broken places in my life were revealing God to me in new and deeper ways. He was making me more sensitive to the heartache around me.

He was providing me with the compassion to help others with broken lives. Because of the comfort and the peace I experienced, I could offer them support and direction in their time of need. I learned of God's provision, sustenance, and healing power, whether the need is physical or emotional or spiritual. I learned to let go of my own pride. I learned He is all I need. No matter what I lack in terms of health or possessions, He is the Provision. No matter how others may let me down by betrayal or injustice, I can depend on Him. He is always faithful, He is always there.

I am now experiencing a deeper prayer life than when I first prayed to know Him better, but all along, before I recognized it, He was answering my prayer.

I wonder how often we think God isn't answering our prayers when we are simply not recognizing His answers. And when we pray for rain, a little mud may be necessary.

Victory Over Anxiety

by Sue Foster

LAGUNA NIGUEL, CALIFORNIA

I'm a worry wart. My stubby fingernails testify to this. Some people possess calm, easygoing temperaments. These fortunate individuals aren't easily rattled. Not so with me, for I'm the high-strung, nervous type. "Anxious" should be my middle name.

One morning in August, I woke up as usual to *The Connection*, a favorite Christian radio Bible study program. Occasionally when I felt groggy, I dozed in and out, only catching part of the message. This morning, however, my ears perked up when the topic Winning the War With Anxiety was announced. The in-depth message was based on Philippians 4:6–7: "Do not be anxious about anything, but in everything, by prayer and petition, with thanksgiving, present your requests to God. And the peace of God, which transcends all understanding, will guard your hearts and your minds in Christ Jesus."

No slumbering for me this day! I gave Pastor Skip Heitzig my complete attention. His message was powerful, resonating with me as I agreed that worrying, like a rocking chair, gives me something to do but doesn't get me anywhere. Hmm . . . now that's an interesting statistic—only 8 percent of what we worry about actually comes to pass. One cogent point, "worrying is not becoming of a child of God," seared my conscience. Yes, if I truly trust the sovereign God is in control of my life, I have no excuse to fret, I confessed. Instead, I must choose to cast all my cares upon the Lord and then rest in Him. For God is more than able to handle my problems and concerns.

At the conclusion of the broadcast, I jotted down the ordering information, intent on purchasing a cassette tape of this relevant message. I promised myself I'd place the order within the next day or so.

Days, weeks, and months slipped by. By then, the note was buried under several books and other scraps of paper on my nightstand. One evening in early December I was possessed by a sudden impulse to tidy my nightstand. The long-forgotten note resurfaced. "Well," I mused, "if I haven't bothered to order the tape by this time, I suppose I never will." Crumpling the note, I tossed the wad into the bedside wastepaper basket.

Bright and early the next morning I tuned in as usual to *The Connection*. As it turned out, the most popular shows of the year were being rebroadcast that month. The radio announcer intoned, "This morning we will be airing Winning the War With Anxiety." I practically fell out of bed! Guiltily retrieving the note from my trash can, I uttered a prayer to God. "Lord, if this is not a crystal-clear message from you, I don't know what is! I promise I'll order the tape today."

Upon receipt, I listened to the tape several times, resolving to take the lesson points to heart. Of course, old habits die hard.

Several weeks later, as I was sorting out the bills from the bulk of the mail, I realized that one bill was missing. The Department of Motor Vehicles registration renewal on my car had disappeared. In vain, I searched through the stack of mail three or four times. Then in my usual manner, I began to worry.

That evening at bedtime, I brought up my concern to my husband. "Steve," I fretted, "I don't know what to do. I don't remember the amount due, or the due date. All I remember is the bill is due sometime in January. Should I call the DMV? I doubt I'll get to speak to a live human being. Instead, I'll probably be connected to one of those annoying automated menus. Press 1 for such-and-such, press 2 for whatever—"

"Sue," my husband broke in, "your agitated state is stressing me out. It's bedtime, and I want to be at peace. Give your worries to God."

"Do not be anxious about anything, but in everything, by prayer and petition . . ." flashed through my mind. Meditating on this verse, the truth that I possessed the power to choose my response to problems finally sank in. I could choose to be anxious, or with God's help I could elect to be at peace. Resting my head on my pillow, I began to pray. *Father, I choose not to fret about this problem any longer. Rather, I shall rest in you, as I commit my concern to your care. Lord, if you're willing, please locate my misplaced bill and restore it to me. Thank you. Amen.* Within minutes, I fell asleep.

The next morning, after a peaceful night's sleep, I searched through the mail stack again. Painstakingly I examined each and every bill with no luck. Five minutes later, on a whim, I decided to check through the mail one last time. Halfway through the stack of bills, the misplaced invoice suddenly reappeared! I could hardly believe my eyes. In amazement, I prayed, *Wow! Lord, you are so awesome! Thank you for answered prayer!* Divine intervention was obviously at work here! Then I added, *Lord, you have just taught me a powerful lesson relating to Philippians 4:6–7. This scripture shall serve as my guide and companion in the new year.*

Evidently God desired to confirm His message to me. In his last sermon of the year, our pastor addressed the subject of worry. He quoted from the Bible where Jesus exhorts His followers not to worry about the necessities of life. If the Father attends to the needs of simple birds and flowers of the field, will He not more so take care of His children's requirements? Our pastor concluded his message with the prayer that we would be worry-free throughout the coming year.

In mid-January a good church friend returned from her trip to South Africa, where she had spent the Christmas holidays visiting her family. She brought back a small gift for me. Knowing that I collect ceramic frogs, she couldn't resist this particular one she came across in a gift shop. The frog is posed in a semi-reclined position, with legs crossed and arms bent. One hand is in its mouth. It sure looks like the frog is biting its fingernails to me. Must be a nervous habit! I'm convinced God has a wonderful sense of humor! And He has found yet another way to reinforce the lesson He is patiently teaching me. I have placed the frog on my greenhouse window shelf in the kitchen. Every single day as I wash the dishes, I am reminded of Philippians 4:6–7. "Be anxious for nothing . . ." Then making a conscious U-turn in my thoughts and attitude, I choose the pathway to peace. In so doing, I change the story of my life.

Meeting Kelly

by Geri Moran
ELMSFORD, NEW YORK

I was at another of life's crossroads, unemployed after losing a job I loved. I was alone, depressed, and feeling I just didn't have the "stuff" to rise to another challenge. I decided to take some of my meager savings and flee to the East Coast for a few days of contemplation. It had always been a calming and healing place for me, and though it seemed frivolous in light of my lack of income, something or someone was telling me to go there.

On my first day there I was drawn to a small local beach in Mystic, Connecticut, where I had never been before. It was an overcast weekday in late August with no one around. I stood by myself overlooking the water, drinking in the quiet, searching for some clarity. I had stood there for some time when I started to feel restless and turned to leave. It was then I noticed another woman on the beach a few yards behind me.

She too was just standing there, peering out over the water in my direction. There was no one else there, we were strangers, but we were sharing a beach—you know, one of those moments when it would seem rude not to acknowledge each other's presence. She spoke first.

"I hope I didn't disturb you," she said. "I just came here to think things out. Is that what you are doing?"

"Yes," I said, "exactly that."

She hesitated momentarily, looked at me pensively, and then began blurting out things, personal things you sometimes can only tell a stranger, shielded with the relief of anonymity. She told me her problems and her fears. Her husband had been unfaithful and now was leaving her. She was middle-aged, getting divorced, and truly terrified.

"I have to get a job. I don't know how to work, I don't know how to be a single mother, what if the car breaks down, and who will fix it? How can I do everything by myself? I am afraid to be alone."

As she poured out her thoughts, I was startled by the fact her fears sounded so familiar—these exact same thoughts had filled my own head years before. When she stopped talking, I told her how I had been through so many of the same fears and I truly understood how much despair she felt. I told her I was the world's biggest coward, but I got through it all.

She asked me all kinds of questions about how I handled this, and how I found out that, and even what I did when my car broke down! She listened with great attention, as I recalled doing so many things on my own for the first time. Like her, I had gone straight from home to marriage and family, never having been alone.

She said she had another hurdle to face—she was waiting for a biopsy result and might have cancer. This broke my heart because she was going through so much at one time. When I told her I myself was a cancer survivor, she seemed incredulous. "You really have had all these things happen to you? But you seem so together; you must just be stronger than me."

"Yes," I said, "I made it through, but I don't think I was stronger than you. It was hard, but I asked for help when I needed it. And you don't take on everything all at once, every day. You do what you can handle, a little bit each day, and eventually it's okay."

After all this talking she told me her name was Kelly. "I know this may sound strange to you and I hope you don't think I am crazy," she said, "but I was here praying to God for answers, and I think God's answer was that He sent you to me."

At that one moment so much became clear to me. "No," I said, "He sent you to me."

"Me?" she said. "How could I have possibly helped you? All I did was tell you my troubles. You are the one who helped me."

I told her how she made me realize everything I had survived, and how far I had come from those troubles. I realized all those things were much worse than what I was facing now, so there was no reason to believe I couldn't pick myself up and get through this stuff, too.

"So I want to thank you for sharing your troubles with me," I said.

Tears came to her eyes, and to mine, and we hugged each other spontaneously, then both of us turned to leave. We each hesitated a bit getting into our separate cars—I think she was wondering the same thing I was: should we exchange phone numbers, keep in touch? But somehow it seemed fitting, as we drove off in different directions, that the only thing we were supposed to keep in touch with was the memory of our meeting. And so I have, and I share it with you.

It was one of those happenings that's too consequential to be mere coincidence. Was it God? I truly believe it was—God, direct, in living color, and in stereo surround-sound.

A Test of Faith

by Susan Kelly Skitt
CHALFONT, PENNSYLVANIA

Two police officers stood on my doorstep. I tried to swallow the lump in my throat. *What do they want?* My husband, Gerry, was at work, and our nine-month-old son, Jared, was taking a nap. Reluctantly, I let the officers inside.

The younger officer shifted uncomfortably while the senior officer asked several questions about Gerry and the car he was driving.

"Mrs. Kelly, your husband's been involved in an automobile accident," he calmly stated.

My heart felt like it was going to jump out of my chest, and I hesitated before I could speak. "Is he okay?" I managed.

"We're sorry to inform you, but Gerry didn't make it."

"No," I stammered. "There must be some mistake."

"I'm sorry, Mrs. Kelly, but your husband died in the accident."

My head was swimming. This couldn't possibly be happening. Desperate, I looked around the room for a familiar face. A strangled whisper escaped my lips. "What do I do? Dear Jesus, I don't know what to do."

In that moment, I knew I had a choice—trust God or reject Him. My husband and I had recently completed a Bible study of Job at church. Job had a choice when his world fell apart. His wife told him to curse God and die, but he didn't. He chose to trust God, even though he struggled.

"Jesus," I screamed, collapsing to the floor, "please help me!"

This was a test of faith, and I didn't know if I was going to make it, but I knew it would be impossible without Jesus. I had trusted Him as my Savior when I was seven years old. He saved me from my sin and promised me a home in heaven. I knew I needed the One who saved me now more than ever.

Jared woke up crying. I raced down the hall and scooped him out of his crib, hot tears stinging my face as I rocked him back and forth. "It's okay, baby. Mommy's here."

Night after night I cried myself to sleep. Without Gerry, I was on my own. All the household responsibilities and obligations fell on my shoulders. Being both Mom and Dad to Jared was exhausting, and when the family room flooded, it was frustrating and humbling to ask others for help.

Through the most difficult moments, I learned to cling to the promise of God's Word: Heaven is my real home. Jesus will never leave me or forsake me. He will take care of me and help me. Don't be afraid.

I was lonely, but God's Word reminded me I wasn't alone. My younger sister, Pam, moved in with me. Family and friends surrounded me with their love and prayed continuously for me. God's strength worked through my weakness, and I was surviving.

One day, while visiting with my grandmother, I asked her about her friend. "Didn't Mrs. Skitt's husband die young?" I asked her. "I'd like to write her a letter." I was desperate to connect with someone who'd experienced the same kind of loss. I didn't know Mrs. Skitt well, but I knew her son, Jim, from youth camp. We used to play Ping-Pong and volleyball together.

The last thing I expected was a response, but I soon found myself sitting at my grandparents' table across from Jim. I hadn't

Choosing to Triumph

seen him in years, and he had recently moved back to the area.

"Jim's here to give us some help with our church sound system," my grandfather explained.

During the weeks ahead, Jim and I crossed paths numerous times at church.

"I was touched by your letter," Jim told me one day. "So was my mom. It brought back a lot of memories for us."

Jim and I started spending more time together. He walked me through my pain and grief, even though it was difficult for him, too. He cried with me and laughed when we remembered our days at camp. He made me feel alive again.

In time, our friendship turned to love and marriage. Jim has been a caring, loving, and understanding father for Jared. We were also blessed with another son, Joel, and Jared is thrilled to have a brother.

Even after all these years, the pain of loss is still there, but it's different. My life is different. I love Jim and the family God has given us, but there is a part of me that will always miss Gerry. He was my high school sweetheart, my husband, Jared's father, and my friend.

Life has indeed been hard, but God is good. Jesus says in John 16:33, "These things I have spoken to you, that in Me you may have peace. In the world you will have tribulation; but be of good cheer, I have overcome the world" (NKJV).

I don't understand why God chose this path for me, but I know I can trust Him. He's the One who gives me strength for today and hope for my tomorrow.

Purpose of Life

by Patricia S. Toornman Bales

BRIGHTON, COLORADO

I looked around the classroom. I was the last one to leave again. I just didn't want to go home to an empty house. Every day seemed the same. There wasn't much use in cooking dinner for just one. The house stayed clean with only me there. There wasn't much noise anymore. I had never been an avid television viewer, so the house was always quiet.

It was just an empty, lonely house.

So often I cried out to the Lord. What is my purpose in life now? Is that all there is? I knew what my purpose had been. Hadn't I lived as a faithful servant, praying diligently as I fulfilled my purpose? I loved the Lord, but now it seemed I was in despair. I felt all alone.

I had been divorced for twelve years. My boys were young, twelve, eight, and six, when their father left and didn't look back. The times he saw them were few and far between, giving me very little downtime. I basically raised them by myself.

I used to tell them, "Your father divorced me, that doesn't mean I will ever divorce you. We're here for the long haul together."

The boys knew they were the most important people in my life and that I loved them very much. We did everything together. I was the active parent who was at every swim meet, every Boy Scout function, and every school conference. Working full time, and with three very active boys, I kept busy—too busy. I didn't make time for my own friendships and my own hobbies.

Then my last son went off to college. Exit: Involvement and filled time. Enter: Uninvolvement and empty time.

It wasn't that my boys didn't phone home regularly. They did, and I'm sure they would have called more often if they had known how lonely I was. I didn't tell them. It didn't seem fair to have them feel guilty over how I was feeling. It was their time to go out into the world and be on their own, not take care of me. I hid this feeling of depression from them. Every time they called I would cheerfully say I was fine.

It didn't help when menopause reared its ugly head the year my youngest went off to college. Physically my body was putting on the brakes. Where I used to stand, I preferred to sit now. My robust zip turned to a weak zap. I felt as if someone turned on the heat and the air-conditioning at the same time. I couldn't keep my toes and fingers warm even when having a hot flash. I had started life out like a lightning flash, fast and dazzling, but had slowed to a fading glimmer.

Once again I asked, "What is my purpose in life now, Lord?"

Opening the door into my house I looked around. It was the same today as it was a year ago when my boys were home, though now it was quiet. I remember longing for quiet when life was so packed. Just a few minutes of it seemed so precious. I opened the refrigerator. Too often in the past, whatever I was looking for had already been eaten. Now I was in charge of all I saw. Though it wasn't packed as it had been in times past, it had everything I liked.

I looked at my watch. It was time for the news. I had never taken the time to watch the news because I was too busy. Now if I wanted to I could. Going to the bathroom I didn't have to make sure the toilet lid was down. It just was. Looking in the mirror, I stared at the reflection looking back at me. That had changed. There were lines around the mouth and eyes I didn't remember from yesterday. Yet that wasn't what was bothering me.

The biggest change was there was no longer a smile. I tried smiling. I looked younger when I put a smile back on my face. The lines all seemed to belong with a smile. I went to the kitchen table, where I had left my Bible from this morning. I was reading through the Bible and had just started Ephesians. I reread the first chapter. "In him we were also chosen, having been predestined according to the plan of him who works out everything in conformity with the purpose of his will" (Ephesians 1:11).

My purpose—His purpose. I was focusing a lot on the "my" instead of the word "purpose." Maybe there was more to the word purpose. *Webster* defines it as, "to put before oneself as something to be done or accomplished; an intended or desired result, end or aim."

Isn't that just what I did when it came to raising the boys? My purpose, for what seemed a lifetime, was to raise my boys. I had done a good job, as all three were well-adjusted, excellent young men. Maybe I was only thinking of myself instead of the real purpose God wanted.

I am a teacher. Each year my purpose is teaching my students the curriculum so they will be ready for next year's teacher. When June comes around and they have passed to the next grade, my purpose has been completed. Yet there will be another year and another new group of students, another purpose.

I sat down and got out a piece of paper. On one side I put things I had already accomplished, on the other side I put things I would

Choosing to Triumph

still like to do. Of course the former was filled quickly with raising my boys and fulfilling that goal. The other side was harder to fill out.

At first everything related to my family. I would have three weddings. Someday I would hold my grandchildren in my arms. I had already attended one of my boys' graduation from the Air Force Academy and then medical school; the others would follow with their degrees. I still had years of teaching. I had a few people I had always put off spending time with because I was too busy. I could cultivate friendships now. I had always wanted to volunteer at women's shelters and never had the time. The list started to grow. There still could be purpose in my life.

I called one of the people I hadn't seen in a long time and made a dinner date for later in the week. Then I fixed what I wanted for dinner and turned on the news and ate while I watched TV. I highlighted some of the things I would do immediately and hung my list on my refrigerator. I went into the bathroom and looked in the mirror. I looked healthy as my cheeks were rosy from a hot flash, and it made me smile.

"Therefore we do not lose heart. Though outwardly we are wasting away, yet inwardly we are being renewed day by day" (2 Corinthians 4:16).

There was still purpose in life. I only needed to realize the Lord knew what His purpose for me was. All I needed to do was choose those things according to His will.

Do You Want to Get Well?

by Cindy Powell

REDLANDS, CALIFORNIA

"Do you want to get well?"

The words leapt off the page of my Bible. I knew that was the question the Lord was asking me. Did I want to get well? Of course I did—didn't I? Wasn't it obvious? Wasn't it what I was asking Him for?

It was Sunday morning, and it had already been an intense weekend. The Single Mom's ministry I was involved with held a day retreat on Saturday. It was not an easy day. I must have slept in an awkward position the night before, because I woke up with an intense pain in my shoulder and neck. But the physical pain was only a small reflection of the much deeper pain in my heart.

Throughout the day, my friend Deb, who led the ministry, kept throwing concerned glances my way. Somehow I kept it together through most of the day, but finally I couldn't hold back any longer. I stole away from the group and broke down in deep, gut-wrenching sobs.

The torrent of emotion began earlier in the day. The retreat was held in a beautiful garden paradise. During the afternoon, we were instructed to find a little corner among the individually themed gardens to spend some time in quiet reflection with the Lord. Without realizing it, I wandered straight into the Garden of Healing. Being there frightened me, so I moved on. With its cheerful and playful motif, I walked over to the Garden of Childhood Memories, but just as I sat down, a swarm of bees decided to join me. That wasn't the kind of company I was looking for! I went next to the Garden

Choosing to Triumph

of Reflection. I thought to myself, *This must be it!* It was both beautiful and peaceful—until half the women at the center noisily decided to pick the same spot! I was beginning to get restless—wandering in circles.

No matter how many times I tried to avoid it, I kept finding myself right back in the middle of the Garden of Healing. Finally, with a shrug of my shoulders and a loud sigh, I sat down. "I give up, Lord—if you want me to stay here, I will."

Tears began rolling down my cheeks as soon as I sat. I knew the Lord wanted to touch a deep area of my heart, and I was terrified. I cried out to Him, "It's too hard! I don't want to remember! Please just leave me alone!" I was paralyzed by fear. I knew staying in this garden meant facing a depth of pain I wasn't sure I could bear. Finally the still, small voice of my Savior quieted my soul. "Beloved, I didn't bring you here to destroy you—I brought you here to heal you. Will you trust me?" It took every ounce of my strength to be still. I wanted to get up and run and never look back. But I had come to love and depend on the One who spoke those words. I was learning to trust Him. So I stayed.

I had been afraid for as long as I could remember. I lost my father when I was just nine and, soon after, lost my innocence at the hands of two very sick and abusive men. For years I survived—rather than lived—with a huge fortress around my heart. The pain and fear was so much a part of me it became my identity. It was who I was.

Until I met Jesus. I had given my life to the Lord a few years before the retreat. His piercing gaze of love melted my defenses and began to heal my broken heart. Never had I experienced such pure love and such complete acceptance! As I grew closer to Him, I knew

I wanted to be whole. I wanted to be all He created me to be. But was it too late? Had too much been lost?

As the Lord began to peel away the layers of pain surrounding my wounded heart, the memories became more intense. My resistance grew stronger. My fears began to increase. What else was lurking in the basement of my heart? What would it cost to face the secrets I had long ago locked in the depths of my soul?

After the other women left the retreat center, Deb found me. She just held me and let me cry. "The Lord is doing a deep work in you—He'll carry it out to completion." I desperately wanted to believe those words, but I still wasn't convinced.

That night I took a walk. I was still one big churned-up mess of emotions. But somehow, in a rare moment of courage, I drew a line in the sand. I made a decision—and a vow. "No matter what it costs, no matter how long it takes, no matter what I have to face, I want to be healed! I want to be whole! And Lord, if you promise to help me, I promise not to run away from you—ever!" I didn't know what that promise would cost, but for the first time in quite a while, I went home believing there might be hope for me after all. Maybe it wasn't too late.

The next morning as I got ready for church, my heart felt lighter. I had a sense of anticipation—I just knew God was working. I will forever remember the title of my pastor's sermon that day: God Can Free You Up. His text was John, chapter five: the paralytic at the Pools of Bethesda.

"Do you want to get well?" When I read those words I was startled. They were so direct—almost unkind. But I was even more startled by what I read next. My eyes drifted down the page to verse 9,

"At once the man was cured." At once! Immediately! Not after enduring years and years of painful reflection—at once!

My heart soared. Suddenly I understood the Lord's words to me the previous day. What's more, I knew I had already made my choice. "Yes, Lord! I want to get well. This day, this moment, I believe You have made me whole."

My "destination" had been changed the day I accepted Jesus as my Savior—but in one critical moment, my *destiny* was changed. In that moment, I knew I would never again let the past define my future. I knew—whatever the cost—I would fulfill God's purpose for my life. I would be all God had created me to be.

No, it hasn't been easy. Although the healing came in a moment—with a single touch—living it out will take a lifetime. But I made a deal with the Lord that weekend: if He promised to help me, I promised not to run away. He's kept His end of the bargain— and then some. I plan to keep mine.

"Therefore, if anyone is in Christ, he is a new creation; the old has gone, the new has come!" (2 Corinthians 5:17).

Do you want to get well?

choosing to be a friend

Even now my witness is in heaven; my advocate is on high. My intercessor is my friend as my eyes pour out tears to God. —Job 16:19-20

One of the most familiar Sunday school songs is "Jesus Loves Me." Youngsters learn early in life that Jesus is someone who knows us, loves us, and will never leave our side. He is the very best friend we will ever have. As we grow in our understanding of friendship, we learn that not only is He a true friend to us, He is a model of how to be a friend. When we reach out to another person, He can reach out through us. When we hold a hurting friend and pray with them, He is in our midst, consoling and comforting. When we rejoice with a brother or sister, He multiplies the joy. Choose to reach out and let Jesus touch the world through you. Choose to be a friend.

Saving Babies

by Dianna Graveman
ST. CHARLES, MISSOURI

Middle school children are like baby giraffes: clumsy and funny-looking, needy—but eager for independence. It was into this den of awkward innocents I entered one school year, believing I could make a difference.

The first thing I learned as an inexperienced middle school teacher was humility. The kids didn't want my help. They just wanted me to leave them alone. The second thing I learned was persistence. I had to find a way to teach them, and I probably wasn't going to get it right the first time.

Many of these children came from less than desirable home situations. It didn't help that I had recently left an academically accelerated private school, where parental expectations were high and strong discipline was valued. I wasn't sure how to function effectively in this new world.

The middle school was overcrowded, and getting trampled in the hallway was a real possibility during passing periods. The cafeteria was ill-equipped to accommodate all of those students, and many of them spent a good deal of their lunch break standing in line. There were not enough chairs or tables for everyone to sit and eat, and those students left standing often felt like targets for physical and verbal abuse from classmates.

One afternoon, Jeffrey, a boy in my fifth period, asked if he could eat in my classroom. He said he was getting picked on in the cafeteria. Jeffrey was small for his age, but feisty. His dad was in prison, causing much speculation among faculty members, and his mom had been periodically hospitalized for drug addiction. He had four siblings, all younger, and it was unclear who looked after the kids when Jeffrey's mother was sick. Most days Jeffrey came to school needing a bath. Mondays weren't so bad, but by Friday it was a real effort not to back away or make a face when Jeffrey got too close. It was easy to see why he was being picked on.

Jeffrey ate in my room every day after that, and word got around. Little by little, other students who felt bullied began arriving with their lunch trays. The faculty lunch room was also overcrowded, and I really didn't mind spending my lunchtime with the kids. It made for interesting midday conversations. Some days I just sat back and listened, hoping they would forget I was there so I could eavesdrop. Occasionally I gained insight into the lives of some troubled young people.

But these children and their problems began to wear on me. They didn't seem to want to work very hard. They had no real desire to learn. They were too busy trying to survive emotionally to care about essays and chapter tests. Just when I thought I was getting through to one young girl, she prematurely gave birth to a very small baby and left school for the term. Because of her size and style of dress, I hadn't even realized she was pregnant.

So I was disappointed, but not terribly surprised, when Jeffrey was suspended from school for threatening another student. I resigned myself to gathering the work he would miss for the next few days so we could catch up during our lunch period when he returned.

Before Jeffrey's suspension ended, a tragic event unfolded in the national news. A student in California brought a gun to school and shot some classmates. The country had seen a respite from school violence in the post-Columbine days, but now it appeared we were doomed to witness a repeat of those senseless times. Within days, hit lists, threatening notes, and bomb scares began surfacing in middle schools and high schools around the country, and our school was no exception. Most of the threats were believed to be hoaxes, but nobody knew for sure. Fears escalated and emotions were tense. Students began calling home during passing periods, terrified about the latest rumor. Parents showed up in the school lobby to take their kids home. There weren't enough phone lines to meet the needs of anxious parents hoping to receive assurance of their children's safety.

The assistant principal came to school one morning looking very tired. She had lain in bed the night before thinking, "What if I missed *the* one? What if the one I thought was the hoax was for real?" With no hope for sleep, she had trudged into the school building in the middle of the night and worked her way up and down the halls with a master key, opening and inspecting each student's locker. Invasion of privacy would not be an issue here.

Weeks passed, and the only violent acts that transpired at our school that spring were some thrown punches. But now Jeffrey was suspended from riding the school bus—this time for assault. Because he had a diagnosed behavioral disability, the school district was required to provide transportation back and forth for him, so Jeffrey would arrive every day in a cab. This didn't last long before he began to miss a lot of school. Gossip had it that his mom was too hung over most days to make sure he caught the cab, and Jeffrey sure wasn't going to take the initiative.

Toward the end of April, Jeffrey was removed from my student roster. He still came to school periodically, but now I was informed that he had been declared emotionally disturbed after several additional violent outbursts. He would be educated in an alternative setting for children with special needs. He never returned to my classroom. I didn't even get to say good-bye.

My teaching contract for the following year was on my desk, but I couldn't bring myself to sign it. I'd had enough. I checked the box beside the words, *I do not intend to return next school year.*

I grabbed the only piece of paper from my mailbox in the school office and headed for the parking lot. Waiting at a stoplight, I fished the mail from my pocket. It was a handwritten note on a torn piece of loose-leaf paper, etched in a barely legible scrawl:

Dear Miss Graveman,
      Thanks for what you did for my sun, he dint have no one to talk to but you

                                        Dawn Brown (Jeffrey's mom)

I carefully folded the note and put it back in my pocket. The light turned green as I argued with my conscience. "This is not what I need," I thought. "This sure is not what I want."

However, it's what I got. I had spent most of my life skipping from job to job, wondering if God had a plan for me. For a while it seemed like teaching was it; I was being called. But now I had begun to long for those days when I could leave my office job behind at five o'clock instead of carrying the trials and broken lives of troubled children home with me each evening—those days when I could eat my lunch in a quiet restaurant while enjoying a good book, instead of hosting an informal gathering of fifty young people looking to escape the oppressiveness of their crowded middle school cafeteria.

"Maybe this isn't what God has in mind for me forever," I thought, "but it's what He has in mind for me *right now*."

It took me several more stoplights and a lot of self-examination before I made an illegal U-turn and headed back to school. After all, there was still a lot to do if I was going to be ready for those kids tomorrow. Besides, I had a contract to sign.

A Gift of Memories

by Anne Goodrich
KALAMAZOO, MICHIGAN

It was a fair spring day when I picked up my eight-year-old daughter, Kelly, from a playdate at her new friend's house. I stood in the gravel driveway introducing myself and chatting with Karen, the mother, while our daughters squeezed a few more minutes of playtime into a sunny afternoon.

Suddenly a look of recognition washed over Karen's face. "I know who you are!" she exclaimed. I looked at her quizzically. "We were in the hospital together when our daughters were born. Maybe you don't remember me, but I've never forgotten you. I was only seventeen when Molly was born, and I was so scared . . ."

And then I did remember. Instead of the usual joy that accompanies the birth of a child, I felt desolate and lonely in that hospital ward after my daughter was born. I had just had my second child in less than a year and a half's time, I was twenty-four years old, and I felt my marriage was falling apart. My husband visited me in the hospital only about fifteen minutes a day, so I was on my own most of the time to take care of my new baby and observe the three other women who occupied my ward.

I couldn't help but notice Karen, the teenage mother, kitty-corner from my bed. From the nurses' furtive whispers I found out why Karen sat in shock, staring with blank eyes. At seventeen years old she had been unprepared for the thirty-six hours of hard labor she endured. She sat empty and expressionless as her young husband held and cared for their newborn. Limp strands of hair framed her

Choosing to Be a Friend

listless face, and she would only shake her head no when asked if she wanted to hold her baby. Karen appeared devoid of feelings, as though her spirit had ebbed away through the long hours of labor and birth. I felt compassion for this young woman, and empathy as well, as I struggled with my own demons of depression.

I suppose that's why one night, when I suddenly woke at 2 A.M., I immediately looked over at Karen's bedside. Our other two roommates were sleeping peacefully, but in the glow of the nightlight over her bed, I saw Karen was awake. Should I leave her alone, should I try to help?

I pulled on my robe and tiptoed over to her side. "Hi," I whispered. "I'm going down to the nursery to see my baby. Do you want to come with me?"

"I don't even know where it is," Karen hesitantly replied.

"I'll show you."

And so we shuffled slowly down the lit hospital corridor, two young mothers, each with her own fears. I tried my best to help Karen alleviate hers as we talked and walked together to the nursery, where Karen finally held her newborn daughter.

All of these memories came flooding back as I stood in a driveway on a spring afternoon years later, watching our eight-year-old daughters play together. Karen spoke again.

"I don't think you realize how much it meant to me," she said softly. "You came over that night and talked to me and spent a long time helping me get over all the fears I had, and then you walked me down to the nursery to hold my daughter. I've never forgotten you and how you pulled me out of my despair."

As we stood there together, I thought of how having my baby

girl should have been a time of great joy for me, but regrettably, many of my memories through the years had been sad and lonely ones. I felt a wave of love and serenity wash over me, and a humble gratitude that God had allowed me in my loneliness to choose to reach out and help someone else in her pain. The gift of joyful memories Karen felt I had given her was now being returned to me. We had come full circle, with God watching and smiling down at us all.

Emma

by Julie Mathiason-Bendel

FARIBAULT, MINNESOTA

It had been an unusually hectic day, and I was eager for my shift to end. As I sat charting at the nurses' station, I could hear a distant murmur from one of the nursing-home residents.

The night shift had arrived and was beginning to make their rounds. Just one more minute and it would be 11:30 P.M.—time to go home. As I grabbed my jacket to leave, I passed the room where the whimpering originated. It was Emma, an elderly woman who had recently been diagnosed with cancer.

On this particular night Emma had been pushing the call light frequently. Although restless and uncomfortable, Emma wasn't due for pain medication for two more hours. I surmised nothing more could be done for her and continued past her room.

Something drew me back.

Suddenly I found myself standing at Emma's bedside, holding her hand. With the exception of the light peering in from the hallway, her room was dark. Explaining to Emma it was too soon for pain medication, I encouraged her to rest. Before I departed she asked me to pray for her. Although her request took me by surprise, I complied. Still holding her hand, I asked God to take away Emma's pain and allow her to rest peacefully for the remainder of the night.

Emma died several weeks later. Several nursing-home staff members and I attended the funeral. As I introduced myself to Emma's daughters, one of them asked me if I had heard her mother speak of angels. Her daughter said two weeks earlier Emma claimed to have been visited in the middle of the night by a beautiful blond-haired angel dressed in white. She said her room was dark but for a bright light illuminating from behind the angel. Emma claimed to have been in great pain until the angel prayed for her. She told her daughter the pain disappeared instantly and she slept comfortably the rest of the night.

My eyes filled with tears as I listened attentively to this wonderful story. I knew I was her blond-haired angel dressed in my white nursing uniform. Her perception of "illuminating light" was, in fact, the light from the corridor streaming through her open door the night I was inexplicably drawn to her bedside.

Until that time, I never fully understood what people meant when talking about angels on earth. I now realize angels aren't necessarily divine winged beings, but rather, sometimes just His messengers of flesh and blood. What a blessing I received just for choosing to stop by Emma's side and give her comfort.

Dinner With Sinners

by Tonya Ruiz

GARDEN GROVE, CALIFORNIA

"Now it happened, as Jesus sat at the table in the house, that behold, many tax collectors and sinners came and sat down with Him and His disciples" (Matthew 9:10 NKJV).

I was busy with my quiet suburban life and perfect family: one husband, four children, two frogs, and an aquarium full of assorted fish. Although I homeschooled the children, the amphibians and aquatic animals were on their own. Tomatoes and cucumbers grew in the vegetable garden and I received many compliments on the calla lillies blooming in the front yard. When the holidays rolled around, the Christmas gifts and cards were homemade. I cut coupons, wore flower-print dresses, cooked pot roast, and cleaned my house weekly. The Stepford wives had nothing on me.

When our new neighbors moved in across the street, I immediately decided we had nothing in common. We had different lives, different values, and different worlds. Other than a "Hello" and a handshake, I stayed away. I jokingly told myself, "I'm way over quota on friends and neighbors anyway." There was no welcome party, not even a friendly plate of chocolate chip cookies. Nothing.

After playing with their kids, my son came home and told me our new neighbors were planning their wedding. "Oh my, they're not even married?" I asked. Rolling my eyes, I said to my friend from down the street, "My kids definitely won't be playing at their house."

"Welcome to the Hotel California" blared from across the street at their wedding reception.

"What has happened to our neighborhood?" I asked my husband as I spied out my bedroom blinds.

He shook his head and said, "Maybe you should use some binoculars."

"You're right," I said as I rifled through the drawer looking for them. He was in disbelief that I even considered his joke as an option.

The craziness continued until months later when my doorbell rang and there stood my nearly new neighbor. With a desperate look on her face, she asked, "We're having some family problems; do you know of a church we could go to?" I was surprised and ashamed as I stood in a puddle of my self-righteousness.

In all my months of condemning and judging, never once did I consider reaching out to them or having them over for dinner. An invitation to church never crossed my mind. How had I completely ignored my days before becoming a Christian? I had also cohabitated with my boyfriends, been an Eagles fan, and gone to more than my share of parties! What if my friends had said, "We can't take you to our church concert because of your colorful language, overdone makeup, and suggestive clothing"?

I was ashamed of myself. Jesus did not consider himself better than the tax collectors, prostitutes, or other sinners—why had I?

Not only did our new neighbors go to our church, but during that year they both accepted the Lord. We have since moved across the street when we bought the house directly next door to them. We have laughed together and cried together. They have become our cherished friends, only a block wall separates our lives.

My neighbors taught me a valuable lesson. I could not see past the beer cans to their hearts or hear their desperate cries over the loud music, but the Lord did. Because of them, my vision and hearing have been permanently improved. I have put away my binoculars.

On Wings and a Prayer

by Karen Kosman
LA MIRADA, CALIFORNIA

"Lord, if you really want me to be with Cynthia, then please provide a way," I prayed as I drove back to the hospital. Visiting hours were over for the night, but I hadn't been able to shake the feeling I was needed—God wanted me there by Cynthia's bedside.

My best friend had been fighting cancer for over five years. Originally she'd been given six months to live. Friends and family had witnessed miracle after miracle as God answered prayers on behalf of Cynthia.

"Please, Lord, one more miracle." But I sensed deep within me this time the Lord had other plans. After all, hadn't Cynthia been a courageous fighter? Soon the suffering would end.

"Lord," I continued, "thank you for Cynthia's life, and for the many lives her ministry on eating disorders has touched; for her book *Monster Within;* for the seminars she presented to help those struggling with anorexia and bulimia."

I stopped at a red light and thought, *Cancer did not stop Cynthia's ministry. She had seminars for those fighting cancer and raised thousands of dollars to donate for cancer research.*

I remembered how she'd stand before an audience and ask, "How many of you ladies know what a bad hair day is?" Then Cynthia would take off her blond wig, and with reflections from the lights simmering on her bald head, she'd announce, "Let me tell you, this is a bad hair day!" Laughter would break out, and you could feel a bonding take place across the auditorium.

I thought back to a lunch date Cynthia and I had a week earlier. That afternoon we both realized it might be our last lunch together.

"Karen, the tumors are back in my lungs and my bones. I don't want to die. I want to live for David and our sons. But I don't have the strength to fight."

"Cynthia, I know God is in control. He'll take care of David and the boys if He chooses to call you home."

I wanted to help Cynthia, but first I had to ask God to help me accept His will for my friend.

A week later a phone call came—the call I'd been expecting, but hoped would never come. Perhaps my feelings of the end drawing near began at that lunch date, or perhaps it was the Holy Spirit preparing me.

When I answered the phone, Ellen, a friend from church and neighbor of Cynthia, said, "Karen, Cynthia wanted me to call you. They've taken her to Saint Joseph Hospital with pneumonia and other complications."

A short time later I walked through the door to Cynthia's hospital room. Cynthia always had a smile for me.

Once we were alone she said, "Karen, I feel a presence all around me. Does this mean I'm going to die?"

"I don't know, Cynthia, but maybe the presence you feel is of angels. I'm sure when the time comes you'll be able to see them." Then Cynthia slept.

The next afternoon Cynthia was moved to ICU. They had her on oxygen. I stayed with her and her mother. For short spans of time she'd sleep and then would wake up to make sure we were still there.

When I left, she grabbed my hand and said, "Please come back so I can say good-bye."

Now as I neared the hospital I prayed, "Oh God, please use me tonight. Almost there, Lord. Guide me. Help me to get in."

I parked my car and walked by the front entrance where a posted sign directed the public to the emergency room. There a security guard asked me, "Who is it you're visiting?"

"Cynthia McClure, in ICU," I replied. Then she handed me a visitor's pass. Once I reached ICU I went into the waiting area and picked up the phone. "Hi, my name is Karen Kosman. I'm here for Cynthia McClure."

"Come right in."

I found Cynthia awake. She motioned for me to come closer. The nurse said, "She's been having a rough time. She keeps fighting the oxygen mask."

I pulled my chair close to Cynthia's bed and whispered, "I'm here now. You can go to sleep." Lying on her side, she grasped my hand with both of hers and went to sleep without fighting her mask.

A short time later she woke and asked, "Karen, are you okay? Are you comfortable?" I thought, *How like Cynthia to think of others first.*

"I'm fine. I'm just sitting here and praying for you. Rest, I'm not going anywhere." Cynthia smiled, then closed her eyes and slept.

Lord, I prayed, *I praise you. Thank you for guiding me here tonight. Please work your will in our lives. Help Cynthia not to be afraid. Wrap her in your everlasting arms.*

Cynthia let go of my hands, rolled onto her back, and opened her eyes. I saw her lips moving and realized she was praying. She suddenly raised both arms as if she were reaching for someone. I watched as her face transformed into total peace. No fear, no struggle, just acceptance.

Tears streamed down my cheeks as I realized she was seeing the angels. The next day she slipped into a coma.

At Cynthia's memorial, her dad shared, "The night before Cynthia passed away, I fell asleep feeling depressed. I found myself in a meadow. Cynthia ran toward me dressed in a white robe with long, flowing blond curls. 'Cynthia,' I cried, 'I'm struggling.'

"'I know, Daddy. That's why I've come to give you all my courage.'"

After her dad's testimony, I praised God, for He'd answered our prayers and provided one more miracle—the peace and reassurance that Cynthia entered Glory—not alone, but surrounded with angels.

Walking the Walk

by Nancy B. Gibbs

CORDELE, GEORGIA

"Thank goodness it's Friday," I thought, as I prepared to leave my office and head home. My spirits were high. I carried a smile on my face. Joy filled my soul. The previous Sunday, my Sunday school lesson had been based on how we shouldn't turn our backs on a person with a need. Little did I know, before this week ended, I would fail to live up to the lessons I was trying to teach my students.

My children were coming home from college for the weekend, and I planned to leave work early. My day had finally ended. When I opened my office door to leave, there stood a deaf and mute man. Draped across his shoulder was the thick strap of a brown leather bag. He reached inside the bag, pulled out a yellow card, and offered it to me.

The only thing on my mind was leaving and getting home before my children arrived. They would be there any second. I didn't have time to read this man's card that I just knew, without reading, was a plea for help. Without giving it a second thought, I turned him away.

"No, thank you." I motioned while shaking my head. The man pointed to the cross hanging on a chain around my neck, hung his head slightly, and quickly turned to leave. I remembered something I had accidentally left on my desk and rushed back into my office.

The second I shut the door, I felt a sense of despair and shame. I remembered the disappointed expression on the man's face. I clutched my cross and tears filled my eyes. I realized I had just turned my back on a person with a need. I thought about my Sunday school lesson and felt ashamed.

At that moment I felt unworthy to wear the cross representing Jesus' love for the world. I had failed to walk the talk. The words sounded good earlier in the week. I left my Sunday school room with good intentions, but now I failed to practice the very words I had spoken.

I ran out of my office, hoping a fellow employee had helped the man I had carelessly sent away. I asked my co-workers which way the deaf man went. No one knew what I was talking about. They looked at me strangely. It occurred to me they had not even seen the man; he hadn't asked for help from anyone except me. Could God have been testing my faithfulness? Or did He want to make me aware of the selfishness in my heart?

I ran out the front door and looked all around, but the man seemed to have disappeared into thin air. I felt terrible. Instead of going home, I went back into my office. I attempted to regain my composure. I fell down on my knees and briefly prayed for forgiveness. Getting home early was no longer important. I had to find that man!

"Please give me a second chance, Lord," I begged. I grabbed my purse and ran to my car. The Friday afternoon crowd covered the streets and sidewalks. Looking for this man was like trying to find a needle in a haystack, but I had to try. For almost an hour I drove up and down the city streets, searching for a man whom I had seen for only a brief second.

Finally I got a glimpse of his brown bag. He was crossing the street about a block in front of me. I kept my eye on him while he went into another place of business. I parked, got out, stood beside my car, and waited for him to come back outside. I was holding a few dollars.

Our eyes met as soon as he exited the building. I pointed to my cross and in sign language told him God loved him. For a few seconds the hustle and bustle of the crowd and the cars zooming down the street became quiet. The sick feeling in my stomach subsided.

Even though no audible words were spoken, our hearts were connected for a few seconds. He smiled, took the money from my hand, and nodded. I helped this man monetarily, but he helped me even more by accepting the gift and allowing me to correct the mistake I made earlier.

I made a choice right then and there: If I was going to accept the gift of salvation from Christ and wear His cross around my neck, I had to not only talk the talk, but also walk the walk every day of my life. Fortunately, God gave me the opportunity to right my wrong and the second chance I so desperately needed. My weekend would have been ruined had God not given me a fresh start.

Talking the talk is important. Others need to hear about God's loving mercies. But walking the walk is much more significant. A true Christian shows what he is by what he does with what he has. And let's face it, everything we will ever have comes to us from a loving and generous God. Shouldn't we be willing to share it?

Lessons of a Lifetime

by Elaine Ingalls Hogg

SMITH'S CREEK, NEW BRUNSWICK, CANADA

It was the 1930s, and the people who lived in the tiny island village struggled to provide food and shelter for their large families. Fishing, the main livelihood for those living on the island, was poor—the fish were scarce. Survival became the focus of the whole village.

The new pastor of the small church was concerned about the children. They needed someone to spend time with them and teach them God's ways. One Sunday morning he announced he would like to start a Sunday school class and he needed a teacher. All the mothers in the congregation shook their heads. "Don't ask us to take on more," one mother declared.

"We don't have time to prepare the lessons, and we definitely have no extra money to buy the quarterly Sunday school teacher's guide," they commented.

There was only one person left to ask—Lila, a spinster with no children of her own. The pastor wasn't sure how well she understood children, but he had exhausted all his other sources.

From the kitchen window, Lila watched the pastor make his way up the path toward the house. She had her answer ready. She'd tell him providing for herself and her aging mother at the local fish factory was a full-time job and taking on a Sunday school class with no money for materials was too big a challenge.

"Miss Shepherd, you have an opportunity to make a difference in these young lives," the pastor reminded her before she could give her prepared answer.

"I'll try it for one or two Sundays while you look for someone else," she quickly responded, much to her own surprise. Later she watched the pastor's back as he retreated down the footpath leading to the road below the house.

"What have I done? I don't know how to teach children! This is an opportunity to make a difference," she repeated under her breath as she turned to light the kerosene lamp and prepare her mother's tea before bed.

The first Sunday she taught the story of Jacob and his sons who became the leaders of the twelve tribes of Israel. To make sure the children remembered, she assigned each child a tribe's name. The children went home and told their parents they were now to be known as Reuben, Joseph, or Benjamin. They were excited about learning, so Lila volunteered to stay on as their teacher. She encouraged her young students to memorize verses, and she worked to make each class memorable. She taught the names of the books of the Bible by making up a rhyming verse, and when the children could recite all their memory texts, she gave them a reward.

Although there was little money to buy these gifts, the children were pleased with the little Scripture cards. Sometimes they received small homemade gifts of candy or flowerpots made from decorated tins.

The years passed by and the children grew to be teenagers. War came and called many of them to serve in faraway lands. Others left to study, marry, and seek jobs on the mainland. Eventually Lila left her home, too. In fact, the island became uninhabited except for a couple of summer visitors and a hermit.

However, Lila's influence on the lives of her class stayed with those students. When the members of that Sunday school class heard she was about to celebrate her one-hundredth birthday, they came from near and far to honor her. Fifteen gray-haired and balding senior citizens came to pay tribute to the lady who had taught them more than sixty years before.

Little did Lila know when she chose to volunteer to give classes for just "one or two" Sundays, she would make such an impact on their young lives. The lessons had lasted a lifetime.

CHAPTER four

choosing to pray

"I prayed for this child, and the Lord has granted me what I asked of him. So now I give him to the Lord. For his whole life he will be given over to the Lord." And he worshiped the Lord there. —1 Samuel 1:27

This is part of Hannah's explanation to Eli concerning her son, Samuel, who grew to be one of the most beloved prophets in Israel. In her pain, she turned to God, even though bitterness attacked her heart from the torment she endured from her husband's other wife. Now, that "husband's other wife" part would be enough to cause bitterness and pain, but add to that not being able to have children while the other woman produced in plural. But Hannah knew Who could help her, Who could comfort her, Who could champion her. She also knew to celebrate the Giver over the gift and leave it all in His most capable hands. Hannah is a sister who has blazed a trail of righteousness for us, setting an example for all women. When the going gets tough, forget about getting tough along with it. The smart woman prays it through.

Two Carloads From Peru

by Janet Carpenter
ATLANTA, GEORGIA

"Borrow phone? Please, ma'am."

The nervous words behind me snapped me out of my own little world as I planted three flats of pansies in my side-yard flower garden. It was a gorgeous fall day in Atlanta. It felt good digging in the dirt and breathing the crisp, dry air. We live on a corner lot with traffic on two sides, so I had not paid attention to passing cars or noticed the young woman as she approached.

"Flat tire," she explained in strained English.

"Do you need to call someone to come help you?"

She nodded.

"I'll get the phone for you."

I took the portable telephone to her car and met her mother, seated in it. We smiled and gestured, as her mother did not speak English.

"Where are you from?" I spoke to the younger woman.

"Peru," she answered, holding up her purse with the word "Peru" artfully embroidered on it.

She began calling everyone she knew. Her father was not home. None of her relatives or friends could be reached. The women's faces became more downcast.

I began mentally surveying my own neighborhood. My husband was playing golf and would not be home for several hours. One neighbor was in London, two others were out of town for the weekend, and one was on an oxygen tank. There was not an able man anywhere who could help. It was late Saturday afternoon, so the local service stations were closed.

With a sinking fear in my stomach, I suggested we try to change the tire ourselves. The very thought of trying to jack up a car was scary. Two elderly women and an inexperienced young one had no business fooling with nuts and bolts. Automobile technology is as foreign to me as this woman's language.

We opened the trunk and tried to take out the little spare tire. The bolt holding it would not budge. We used every tool I could find in my husband's shop, prying, hitting, pulling, pushing, and spraying with lubricant. Nothing worked. With busted knuckles and broken fingernails, we had to admit defeat and accept our helpless state.

"Are you a Christian?" I asked.

"Oh, yes!" came her quick reply.

"Well, I believe in prayer. Why don't we pray for help right now?"

She agreed and said something to her mother. The three of us stood at the back of the car with our hands on the trunk as I prayed aloud.

"Lord Jesus, we love you. We belong to you. We know you love us and have promised to supply all our needs. We need help now. We can't change this tire ourselves. We ask in faith, believing. Thank you ahead of time for what you are going to do for us. In Jesus' name we pray. Amen."

"Amen," responded the two Peruvian women.

I sighed. "Well, I'll go get the yellow pages, and we'll start trying

Choosing to Pray

to call for some kind of roadside assistance. I don't know what else to do. Do you?"

"No," the younger woman answered sorrowfully, shaking her head.

I went inside, taking a few minutes to locate the rarely used telephone book. As I brought it outside, I stopped abruptly. Two carloads of people, mostly men, had parked and swarmed around the crippled car. They already had the little spare tire out of the trunk and the car jacked up.

One was motioning to the others. "Go on. I can handle this. Go on, go on! It's no big deal." Reluctantly the other ten men, a woman, and a child loaded up and left, leaving our good Samaritan. He worked quickly on the wheel's lug bolts, speaking kindly to the young woman and her mother in their language. Shortly, the woman and child returned in a car to pick him up. He would accept no compensation from us, only our profuse thanks. Relief showered over all three of us.

"Did you know them?" I asked.

"No."

"Had you ever seen any of them before?"

"No."

"Where were they from?"

Her eyes wide, she lifted her palms in amazement. "All from Peru!"

"What?! All of them? I can't believe this!" I exclaimed. "We must give the Lord thanks."

She nodded.

The three of us resumed our earlier stance, hands on the car, and thanked Him for His incredible answer to our prayers and for His merciful speedy response. We asked Him for a special blessing on the young man who had so kindly helped us.

As we said our good-byes, the mother and daughter conversed in their language—which I, of course, could not understand. Then the daughter spoke slowly and distinctly these words to her mother: "God bless you."

Her mother turned directly toward me, looked me straight in the eye, and slowly repeated, "God bless you." I hugged and thanked her, and I marveled at God's goodness as I waved good-bye.

Yes, God blessed me. Two carloads of helpers, and they were all immigrants from Peru! Isn't it just like the Lord to send more than we can ask or think? Perhaps the two carloads of helpers were already on their way before we prayed. "For your father knows what you need before you ask him" (Matthew 6:8), tells it all. He knew we needed help, but I would never have thought to ask for Peruvian helpers. Now each time I see the blooming pansies in my side yard, I think of God's answers to prayers, and it strengthens my faith.

To God be the glory. Great things He has done!

God's Surprises

by Esther M. Bailey

SCOTTSDALE, ARIZONA

A Christian leader sent out a challenge and desperate plea to our congregation during one of our worship services.

"Many people coming to my seminars have needs I can't meet in the time I have with them. I need prayer partners who will promise to periodically pray for ten people for twenty-one days. In this way we can help more of them."

I quickly volunteered. At first I was so excited I wrote out daily prayers. The trouble with making a commitment under inspiration is keeping the pledge when your enthusiasm goes south. After a while I wondered what I had gotten myself into.

Assignments don't always come at opportune times. They come when I am on vacation, involved in a heavy project, or dealing with a personal crisis. During those times I often forget or make a quick plea: "Lord, encourage everyone on the list. Help them taste the joy of spending time in prayer and in your Word."

God knows each individual by name, but I feel I'm taking the easy way out. Even when I mention names, I find it hard to pray from the heart for people whose specific needs I do not know. To offset my shortcomings, I often extend the period of commitment to compensate for days I missed or prayed in a halfhearted manner.

At the end of the first year, I expected to receive a renewal notice to sign and return if I wanted to continue as a prayer partner. That would give me an opportunity to bow out gracefully.

Five years later, the original commitment still stands. I could ask to be released, but what good Christian would say, "I don't want to pray anymore"?

Occasionally God sends little surprises, making me feel I am doing something worthwhile. I'd receive a note of appreciation from someone I'd contacted or my pastor would say something making me want to continue.

Finally, in November 2000, God sent a big surprise my way. I know God orchestrated the contact because I shouldn't even have received Kathy's name. Always before, I received ten names of people attending the same conference. This time, I received nine names from people in Florida and one from Fredericktown, Ohio—the town where I grew up.

As Kathy and I began to correspond, we bonded quickly. I discovered she was married to a man who had been a child in the church I attended until my early twenties. Kathy also knew my mother and grandmother. With each e-mail we learned something new that strengthened the connection between us. When Kathy was born, I worked for the doctor who delivered her. I may have held Kathy when she was a baby.

At the time we made our acquaintance, Kathy was dealing with the aftermath of tragedy. On June 16, 2000, her father was killed and her mother severely injured in a head-on car crash caused by a drunk driver. Kathy requested special prayer on the day she would face the man responsible for tearing so many lives apart.

Because of the bond between us and the seriousness of Kathy's situation, I became the prayer warrior I wish I could be all the time. On the court date, my heart and mind reached out to God all day no matter what I was doing.

When Kathy reported the details of the hearing, every word she wrote thrilled my soul. "It was totally awesome how the Lord took control and had His way," she wrote.

During testimony, family members revealed their struggle with loss, anguish, anger, and finally forgiveness. After explaining how God helped him through the process, Kathy's son said to the defendant, "I hope someday you can come to know Christ as I have. I forgive you and I'm praying for you."

With a contrite spirit, the man whispered back, "Thank you."

What a great idea, God—church in the courtroom, I thought when I finished reading Kathy's story. I felt blessed to have had a small part in the outcome.

When God gets going on surprises, He doesn't let up. The best was yet to come. Kathy was coming to Phoenix! It was only three weeks until Kathy's arrival, but I felt like a child waiting for Christmas. Days dragged by slowly.

On the appointed day, excitement bubbled inside as I went to pick Kathy up for lunch. I wouldn't have been more thrilled if I had been meeting my favorite celebrity. At first sight, Kathy and I melted into each other's arms. It seemed we had been best friends forever. The charming, vivacious young woman was everything I expected and more.

During our three-hour lunch, my Fredericktown memories surfaced as we talked about mutual friends and familiar places. We discovered we were alike in many ways, such as our taste in clothes, sense of humor, and philosophy of life. For seventeen years she even shared my experience of working for a small-town doctor.

Kathy's loving and forgiving nature showed through her attitude toward the man responsible for her father's death. Tears welled up in her twinkling blue eyes as she said, "I pray for him, and I sent him a letter and a Bible." She grieves because his twelve-year-old son is without a dad while he serves time in prison. In a tender voice she said, "I hope for an early release."

By the time we said good-bye, we formed something akin to a mother-daughter relationship. Ours will be a lifelong friendship nurtured through e-mail, the post office, the phone, and the hope of more face-to-face visits.

So if the seminar leader updates her prayer partners, I will probably volunteer again. God may have another surprise for me, and I wouldn't want to miss it.

Choosing to Pray

Righting a Wrong

by Connie Sturm Cameron
GLENFORD, OHIO

Each year, on my way to and from having my annual physical, I have to drive by the store where it happened—more than fifteen years ago. And with each visit to the doctor, not only do I pray I will get a clean bill of health, but I also ask God to forgive me for what I did in that store. Although I knew I was forgiven the first time I had sincerely asked God to forgive me (Psalm 103:12), I still had a hard time forgiving myself.

That day, fifteen years ago, I had been shopping in a department store and saw two dresses on the same rack that I liked. Both originally had been the same price, but one was now marked down 50 percent. I took the dresses into the dressing room, and after trying on both, I fell in love with the full-priced dress. The problem was, I had just enough money for the sale-priced dress. So while still in the dressing room, I convinced myself the clerks meant to mark down the full-priced dress also, and then boldly proceeded to switch the price tags.

And year after year, when I drove past the store, I struggled anew with my memory. I had never done anything like that before or since, and the guilt was so strong, I could never bring myself to even wear the dress!

But on this trip to visit the doctor, my thoughts weren't about the store and the dresses; I was too concerned about a second breast lump I had recently discovered. It was in the same location as a lump surgically removed the year before, and I was in hopes that this one would also be benign.

What if it is cancer? What if I only have a few months to live?

The closer I got to the doctor's office, the more apprehensive I became. I had assumed since the previous lump had been cancer free, this one would be, also. But what if it wasn't?

Would God bless me with a clean bill of health a second time?

Until now, I hadn't allowed myself to even consider a bad report. Fear began to consume me as I gripped the steering wheel and held my breath.

"God, help me," I cried out loud.

It immediately dawned on me that I had been in such a hurry that morning, I had neglected my quiet time with the Lord. I knew I needed the peace only God can give—but first I needed to ask Him for it.

Father, I prayed, *I am afraid of the worst happening. Please fill me with your peace. I ask that this lump, too, would be benign, but I know you will be with me no matter what the outcome.*

Relaxing my grip, I took a deep breath and placed the outcome into God's hands.

During the examination, the doctor immediately confirmed there was a cyst. "I'd like you to try something this time," he suggested.

"Sure!" I eagerly replied, thrilled at the prospect of no surgery.

"Many times these lumps are caffeine-related, and in some body chemistries, even a small amount can cause benign lumps to form. These cysts, as you know, can be difficult to accurately diagnose without surgery. So no caffeine for six weeks, then come back and we'll see if the cyst is gone."

Ugh.

The first few days were tough—I stopped all caffeine intake, switching to decaffeinated coffee and even giving up chocolate! Miraculously though, within three days I could no longer feel the lump.

Returning to the doctor's office six weeks later, I was thrilled when he confirmed that the cyst had, indeed, disappeared.

"We'll schedule a mammogram as a precautionary measure," he added.

A few days after my mammogram, I walked toward the receptionist's desk. Noticing an X ray clipped to the light panel, I stopped to peer at the image. "Is that mine?" I asked the technician who was standing nearby.

"Oh, no, no, no," she quickly replied, vehemently shaking her head, "and be grateful it isn't. Of course, we'll have to send this off for an official reading, but—it doesn't look good," she added, with a hint of concern in her voice.

Using the tip of an ink pen, she pointed to an off-white glob of cells that my untrained eyes hadn't noticed before.

My feet didn't want to move as I stared at the image of that tiny mass of cells—cells that had the potential to claim a life.

My heart quickly filled with compassion as I realized that very soon, some woman unknown to me but known to God, would be informed her life was about to be drastically altered.

Lord, I prayed silently, *please comfort this woman who will soon be learning she has cancer. Give her the strength and courage she'll need to fight this battle, and please encourage her friends and loved ones to help her through it.*

My lighthearted mood of just moments earlier had quickly

sobered as I got into my car and started for home. I couldn't get my mind off the fact the two cysts I'd had could just as easily have been full of cancer instead of fluid.

Father, except for your grace, that X ray could have been mine. I thank you for my health, and I want to do something to honor you and show my appreciation.

At that moment I stopped at a red light. I gazed over to my right and realized I was beside the store where I had switched the tags long ago.

I knew what I had to do.

I drove into the store parking lot, parked the car, and dug out my checkbook. Already the burden from the guilt of fifteen years was lifting as I wrote out a check for the difference in price of the two dresses, including some extra for interest.

Saying a quick prayer for courage, I went inside and sought the manager.

After I spilled out my story, I tried to thrust the check into a very surprised manager's hand, intent on quickly exiting the store. But the manager didn't want to take it.

Momentarily speechless, she finally said, "This really isn't necessary."

"But you don't understand," I continued, still holding out the check, "I have to right this wrong."

With a huge smile spreading across her face, she finally accepted the check, admitting I had made her day.

I smiled broadly back at her—finally at peace over having done the right thing.

Sitting in my car before leaving the store parking lot, I reflected on that time period in my life when I had switched those tags. I was not a Christian then, but I became one shortly after.

I was suddenly overcome with gratitude at the realization of how I might have lived a selfish life full of misery and regret had I not found God. The list of blessings He has bestowed on me since I began to follow Him seems almost endless.

I began to weep tears of relief and appreciation. I knew I was undeserving of such a happy, fulfilled life, and thanked God for saving a wretch like me. As I started my car, I wiped my eyes and whispered out loud, "But for the grace of God . . . go I."

A Definite Answer

by Betty Z. Walker

FALL RIVER MILLS, CALIFORNIA

As I approached my eightieth birthday, my children became concerned that not only was I alone, but I also did not live near any of them. A very independent person, I'm quite capable of taking care of myself. I knew I didn't want to move in with any of them, but they had a point—it might not be a bad idea if I were closer to one of them.

One of my daughters lived in Northern California, and she and my son-in-law were celebrating their twenty-fifth wedding anniversary and invited me down from Oregon for the event. While there, she encouraged me to look at the house next door to theirs; it was for sale and she thought it might be perfect for me.

Why, this is a lovely home, I thought, and how nice it would be to live next door to my family. But what about my current home? How long would it take to sell? Would I get a good price?

Returning home to Oregon, I chose to turn the whole matter over to the Lord. As a widow, I had no husband to consult, but I knew the Lord would take care of me.

"Lord," I prayed, "if you want me to move, please bring me a cash buyer for my house." I knew that having the cash up front would make the sale quick and approval guaranteed.

I called a Realtor and the For Sale sign went up on a Friday. "It's in your hands now, Lord," I said, as peace filled my heart.

Lo and behold, by Saturday I had a cash buyer! How much more definite could the Lord be in answering my prayers and directing my path toward California?

The family all agrees the Lord could not have made a better arrangement for us. We all praise God for how quickly and wonderfully He answered my prayer. With the money I received for my house in Oregon, I was able to purchase the house right next door to my daughter, where I still live today.

It was a choice that while difficult to make initially, was one of the best choices of my life. I thank God for His provision, and in these twilight years of my life, I rest in the knowledge that He is always in control.

The Woman Next Door

by Brenda Sprayue
MARION, INDIANA

"Not her again." I sighed and quickly stepped away from our window. I was alone in our new home in Chicago, and our next-door neighbor, Nora, was coming up the driveway. When the door-bell rang, I refused to answer it. I didn't want to give this woman another chance to cause trouble.

Hearing the screen door slowly creak open, I detected a rustling sound and a tiny clink. Was Nora messing with my doorknob?

I considered calling the police, but then the screen door creaked shut. I waited a few minutes before cautiously opening the door. A white plastic bag was looped over the handle. Inside was a bag of colorful taffy and a card reading *Happy Halloween*.

Probably poisoned, I thought, and tossed the candy "evidence" into a cupboard. I was convinced my new neighbor was a threat to my family.

I met Nora on my four-year-old Wesley's first day of school. Because we lived on a busy road with no sidewalks, I was disappointed to learn the bus would stop for him a block away. I gripped his small hand, and we walked along the edge of our new neighbor's lawn. The speeding traffic scared me, but I was reluctant to walk any farther onto my neighbor's yard.

When I met the bus after school, *she* was waiting. Nora flew out her door yelling unintelligibly. *There's something really wrong with her,* I thought. As I led my son quickly away, I caught a few words and realized her problem: We were in her yard.

I looked in amazement at the barreling traffic and my sweet little boy. "Where would you like us to walk, ma'am?"

She howled out words like "wall" and "beer cans."

She was *definitely* crazy. "It's okay," I called, unable to leash my sarcasm. "We'll just walk in the street. Thanks so much! Pleasure meeting you!"

At home I shed angry tears. Why did we have to move next door to a cranky old woman? A call to the school secretary calmed me. She said that legally, Nora was out of line. "But we'll have the bus stop at your house from now on."

Nora struck again three days later. My family and I were getting into our car when we heard shrieking. We turned to see Nora storming up our driveway, rapidly taking pictures of all of us with a camera. When she reached my husband, Brian, she got right in his face and snapped a picture.

With amazing restraint, Brian strode to the end of the driveway. Nora followed. "Excuse me," he interrupted. "I don't even know you. Why are you doing this?"

Soon the photo session—and her shouting—stopped. When Brian came back and joined us in the car, he quietly said, "That woman is nuts. She thinks we've been doing all these weird things to her. I told her we just moved in. She doesn't believe me!"

The next day Brian discussed Nora with a police officer he knew. "You could report her," he replied, "but I don't advise it. You'd probably start a war, and if she really is unstable, it could get nasty."

Those words were less than reassuring to me. I imagined a chain of events so hideous they had *Dateline Exclusive* written all over them. I envisioned her terrorizing my family . . . setting the house on fire . . . framing us for child abuse . . . I could see her holding up the pictures she took of our bewildered faces to TV cameras and declaring, "They seemed normal to me."

Such was my state of mind when I met our other neighbor across the street. Sandy had seen Nora's attack from her window and came over to talk to me.

"We've known Nora for nine years, and we've never seen her like this," she said. "She lost her mother last month. The people who lived in your house before you were awful. We talked to her and found out she actually thought you *were* that family."

"Did she *look* at us? Didn't she see any big moving trucks?"

"I guess not," said Sandy. "The last family had kids about the same age as yours. When we finally convinced her you'd just moved in, she cried. She was so embarrassed. She wants to apologize."

I hoped Nora would just stay away from us.

But then Nora left the taffy at my door. After I threw the colorful candy into the cupboard, I called Sandy. She explained, "Nora doesn't hand out treats on Halloween night, but she gives the neighbor kids taffy. Isn't that sweet?"

I wasn't ready to release my paranoia. In subsequent days, I warned my kids to not put one foot in her yard.

"I don't even want to *look* at that mean old lady's house!" my eight-year-old daughter, Kayla, said one day. Sadly, I realized she'd caught my attitude. It wasn't good for her, and it wasn't good for me. I had to do something to turn this around.

It occurred to me I'd been praying only simple, shrug-it-off prayers such as, "Help me forget that nasty woman." I hadn't let the

Holy Spirit get anywhere near my heart and quiet my negative attitude.

"Okay, Lord," I prayed. "How should I choose to respond to this?"

The first verse coming to mind was obvious. "Love your neighbor as yourself." I was familiar with the verse from Matthew 19:19, but the original use of it in Leviticus 19:18 contained a few more words I needed. The first part of the verse cautions us to not "bear a grudge." Yes, my issues had developed into a grudge.

How could I possibly choose to love Nora as I love myself? Well, I certainly always want the best for me. And I don't hold grudges against myself. In fact, most of the time, I'm downright lenient with my shortcomings.

When I behave badly, I'm pretty quick to make excuses . . . a bad hair day, PMS, a loud upbringing. All in all, if I were to love Nora as I love myself, I had to choose to overlook her failures. Wow, did this open my eyes! I could relate to overreacting from fear or stress. And wasn't I acting a little crazy myself this week, hiding from Nora, obsessing over things that would never happen?

I was thankful I'd worked through my feelings and chose to accept Nora for the good neighbor she was. Though we didn't suddenly become best friends, there was never a hint of a problem between us again. We chatted at the mailboxes and waved as we worked in our yards. And as is usually the case, the kids took their cues from me. They always had a polite word and a smile for the woman next door. There was peace, respect, and a very noticeable absence of worry. And, of course, a bag of rainbow taffy every Halloween.

choosing to take a stand

Then Esther sent this reply to Mordecai: "Go, gather together all the Jews who are in Susa, and fast for me. Do not eat or drink for three days, night or day. I and my maids will fast as you do. When this is done, I will go to the king, even though it is against the law. And if I perish, I perish."

—Esther 4:15-16

Queen Esther broke the law and risked her very life choosing to take a stand to protect her people. But in her heart, and in God's eyes, she knew it was the right decision to make. Many times in our lives we may be called upon to take a stand without knowing what the outcome might be. But anything done by God's guidance is in His hands and is safe for eternity. If we trust in knowing what is right and true, and we follow His Word, God will put our true treasure where moth and rust cannot destroy. Our faithfulness will not go unrewarded.

No One Will Know

by Jennifer Devlin
MADISON, ALABAMA

The restaurant was busy as I waited for my friend. Was she coming or not? Twenty minutes went by before I finally went ahead and got a seat. I waited twenty more minutes before ordering food. It was obvious I was by myself.

A guy walked by, smiling, and gestured a polite hello. I was young, single, and didn't have any reason not to talk to him. He was the cutest guy in the room, and his eyes were looking at me, so I decided to take a chance.

"Hi, what's your name?" The usual introductions began. I invited him to sit at the table with me; after all, there was room! We talked about the weather, our hobbies, our jobs, and whatever else came to mind. He was nice, had a good job, and seemed interested in a lot of the same things. We talked about so many things, but I had no idea how important the things we *didn't* talk about were. It didn't even cross my mind to ask him about his faith, if any, or his values, morals, or family life. We were just talking. . . .

"Why don't we get out of here and go to my house—it's too noisy here now," he suggested.

Sounded perfectly fine to me . . . after all, I was young, single, and didn't have any reason not to talk to him. What would God say about my following him home? At that moment, I hate to admit that I didn't really care. It's a good thing God cares about us, even when we don't seem to care about Him.

Before we left, my new friend excused himself for a minute. He walked across the room to talk with a man he seemed to know really well. I didn't realize he had come into the place with anyone else, but at this point, it didn't faze me. As he moved his way back to our table, he flashed the sweetest grin. Taking my hand, we walked out the door, each of us getting into our own car. I followed him to his house—at least I thought it was his house.

Once we had parked and gotten out of our cars, he had a more nervous look than before. "This key is always hard for me to work in this door," he muttered as he struggled with the lock on the front door of the townhouse. He seemed to be anticipating more than just spending time with a new friend. He seemed jumpy.

"You should really get that fixed," I teased.

He huffed with a halfway sarcastic laugh. Looking over his shoulder as he opened the door, he said, "I would, but this isn't my house. This is my brother's house—he was the guy I was talking to at the restaurant."

What? His brother's house? Was this guy living with his brother, or was he just up to no good? He said he had a good job and a house . . . so what was the deal here? My mind raced with questions. "Okay, I give—tell me why we are at your brother's house," I bantered.

"Would you rather we go to *my* house, so you can meet my wife and kids?" he said with much too much ease. The grin on his face when he said it haunts me still today. He sauntered over to the couch, fell back, and motioned for me to come over and sit with him. This obviously was no big deal to him. But he didn't seem to realize it was a big deal to me.

Wife? What on earth had he taken me for? What on earth had I done? While we had only talked, I could tell his intentions were for much more than cozy conversation. Did I really look like a girl who would sink to being the other woman? Surely I had carried myself with more class than that. I was so naïve I didn't even know how naïve I was!

"Mister, I don't know who you think I am or what I'd be willing to do with you. Don't you think you should have mentioned the fact you had a wife while we were in the restaurant? It would have saved us both a lot of time and energy."

"Why would I tell you that? You never would have driven over here if I had. Besides, who will ever know? Come on, let's stop talking and start doing what you know I want to do!"

There we were, me, the single girl, and him, the married guy—in his brother's house. Yuck. Everything in me wanted to scream, yell, puke, and run. What a great mess I had let myself get into. His argument that no one would know was a moot point—I would know, God clearly knew, and my conscience would be seared with the guilt of betraying a man's wife.

But now the question was, could I get out of this with my integrity intact? I suddenly cared very much what God would think. There was no question what my choice should be, or what it would be. Once again, I couldn't believe how ignorant I had been to think we were just new friends getting to know one another.

"Buddy, you just don't get it, do you? I am not going to be your other woman, and I suggest you go home and find whatever it is you were looking for there. I'm going home."

I walked out the door as fast as I could, then unlocked my car, slammed the door with fury, and fumed in anger as I pulled away. He was right. No one would have ever known. I think that's part of the reason I was so mad. Creeps like him get away with stuff like that. And I almost fell for it.

The choice was easy in his mind—and easy in mine. There was a big difference between the two choices: mine led to peace after the storm, his led to a life causing storm after storm.

Somehow, even in my anger, I could feel the approval of God shining down on me. I knew God had allowed me to be tested. The choice I made when this manipulative man attempted to rip me away from a right relationship with my Savior stood clearly in my conscience. I felt closer to God than I had in quite some time.

That night was a good lesson for me. The choice I made saved me from a betrayal that could have impacted more lives than mine. I learned just because a guy doesn't have a ring on, doesn't mean he is single. I learned a married man might try to act like he is single to get you to make a choice sending you on a path away from God.

And I learned to hold fast to my faith in God, so I would never make that wrong choice.

How God Spoke to Me

by Nancy Baker

COLLEGE STATION, TEXAS

I'm grateful God would not let me rest when I tried to be dishonest. The burden of my guilt became so heavy I could not bear it. It was a physical presence I could not escape. But I tried. Oh, how I tried.

It began as a small, insignificant incident, then mushroomed beyond all intention or expectation, the way lies often do. I was on a business trip with a colleague, driving a company car. We stopped for lunch at a delightful Cajun restaurant and were anxious to beat the crowd, in a hurry as usual. Jennifer alighted before me and rushed ahead to get a table. When I tried to open the door of the car, it stuck. I pushed harder. No luck. Taking a deep breath, I shoved with all my might. The effort was rewarded and the door flew open, producing a sickening thud.

My stomach clinched. Oh no, I've scratched the door of the car parked next to me. I don't have time for this. I felt like such a dope. This was my first business trip and Jennifer was so self-assured. I didn't want to admit my mistake to her, much less to my boss. So I decided to just ignore it. I figured no one would notice, not right away at least. Lunch consisted of a succulent blackened red snapper, but it tasted like straw to me. My heart sank upon returning to the car. Fluttering in the breeze under the windshield wiper was the note.

Jennifer immediately called the other driver a jerk. "Nancy, you would have known if you had hit his car. That scratch was probably already there, and when he realized we worked for a big company, he saw the chance to get some money." She pointed emphatically at the company logo on the side of the car.

I am so ashamed I did not live up to my principle of owning up to my actions and taking the consequences. Pride! Oh, how hard to humble yourself before those whose respect you yearn.

"Yeah," I agreed.

Thus began the mushrooming. It was rather easy, for I had a witness who would swear I had not done it. It was simply a matter of our word against theirs. So I lied to my boss, then to the risk management person, then to the accountant. With each lie, my burden became heavier. I tried to ignore my growing guilt, rationalizing that it wasn't important.

But it was.

My New Year's resolution had been to read the Bible through before the year ended, using the daily readings suggested in my devotional. When the lying commenced, my shame would not let me face our Lord, not even in His Word. So on the day my guilt became so heavy I could ignore it no longer, I was many days behind.

That day I had been unable to concentrate. I was not capable of thinking of anything but the lie, so I finally confessed—to a dear and trusted friend. She sent me to the Word. I still resisted and offered some feeble excuse about not knowing where to start.

"Just read what you're supposed to read in today's reading," she counseled.

When I picked up my Bible at last, I simply began where I had left off. This is how God spoke to me *five* times that day, knowing what I needed to hear, knowing where I would begin to read.

"Be strong and courageous. Do not be afraid or terrified because of them, for the Lord your God goes with you; he will never leave you nor forsake you" (Deuteronomy 31:6). I memorized this verse and repeated it over and over. Otherwise I would never have gotten the courage to confess to all the people I had lied to.

"Everyone who speaks a word against the Son of Man will be forgiven . . ." (Luke 12:10). I had spoken a lie, and that is against the Son of Man. But God promises to forgive me.

"When you are brought before synagogues, rulers and authorities, do not worry about how you will defend yourselves or what you will say, for the Holy Spirit will teach you at that time what you should say" (Luke 12:11–12). My translation: "Be obedient to me, Nancy, and I will help you do as I ask."

"But then they would flatter him with their mouths, lying to him with their tongues; their hearts were not loyal to him, they were not faithful to his covenant. Yet he was merciful; he forgave their iniquities and did not destroy them" (Psalm 78:36–38). Once again, God assured me of His forgiveness and His mercy.

"The Lord detests lying lips, but he delights in men who are truthful" (Proverbs 12:22). Oh, how I wanted to be a delight unto the Lord.

I could not believe as I progressed from reading to reading that God had more for me. Each Scripture brought greater and greater assurance of God's presence. With His help, I could be honest.

The confessions were not easy. I cried. The risk management person said she was glad to get the story straight, and there were no recriminations. The accountant adjusted her records. My boss said he could not think of a better time (Easter) for a catharsis, a change of heart allowing me to turn back toward God. He even said he was proud of me for my honesty.

I thank the Lord for this experience, for allowing me to make this U-turn. I am grateful that He loved me enough to humble me. I know beyond a doubt that He is ever present in my life and in His Word and will not forsake me.

It's All in the Timing

by Shelly Beach

SPARTA, MICHIGAN

Dan wrapped his arms around me and pulled me close to his chest as tears streamed down my face and stained his shirt. Our eighteen-month-old daughter, Jessica, clung to our legs, trying to insinuate herself into our embrace.

"You can do this, honey," Dan whispered into my ear. "God will be here for you. Trust Him."

His words only made the tears flow harder. The fact was, I couldn't trust God. Not since a sultry summer night three years before, when a rapist had crawled through a window in my parents' home and attacked me in my own bed.

He'd threatened my life and sexually assaulted me before I was able to break free and leap headfirst from my bedroom window. Compared to the other forty women he had attacked that summer, I was fortunate. My physical trauma was minimal compared to the ravaging that dozens of other women and young girls had experienced.

But the attack had left me emotionally shattered. I couldn't sleep at night, and I suffered from recurring nightmares. I was afraid of the dark, afraid of men who resembled my attacker, afraid of elevators, stairwells, parking garages, getting into empty cars . . . the list went on and on. Over the months that followed, I managed to find ways to avoid most of the scenarios that haunted me, but one fear had backed me into a corner. I was terrified to be alone in a house. Particularly after dark.

Dan and I had been engaged at the time of my attack. I was nineteen, and friends teased me that our wedding plans were put into fast-forward so that I could get a live-in bodyguard. They were pretty much right.

In the months after the attack, Dan became my lifeline. He was inexhaustibly patient with my emotional outbursts, irrational behaviors, and illogical fears. From the day we were married, we began planning our lives around my fear of being alone after dark.

New complications arose when Jessica came into our lives. She was nine and a half pounds of bubbling joy. And nine and a half pounds of newfound guilt growing in my heart with each passing day.

It was one thing for me to know my faith in God had been shattered. It was another thing entirely for my child to figure out why her mother went running from the dark at night. We had given Jessica the middle name Faith. Would she grow up believing that faith was just an empty word?

I had pretty much coasted through my first eighteen years of life believing God loved me and had a wonderful plan for my life. This meant, according to my definition, I would live beneath a spiritual umbrella of protection where none of the Big Hurts of Life could actually fall on my head. So for God to have allowed such a horrible thing as a sexual assault to happen to me was a betrayal. He had obviously abandoned me.

I'd never actually spoken those words out loud, but that was how I felt. And I hadn't felt much like doing anything about it until I held my daughter in my arms.

But deep down, at the core of my being, I knew there was a God who was worthy of my trust, and my faith in Him could only exist when it was exercised.

The thought terrified me, and I wrestled with it for months after Jess was born, usually while I was staring into her eyes as I taught her the words to songs like "Jesus Loves Me" or "My God Is So Big."

Jessica grew to be a year old, and the struggle in my heart continued. Then one day Dan came to me with an announcement. He might as well have handed me a giant placard inscribed with the words, *Your Challenge From God.*

"I want to go back to graduate school for the summer, Shelly. For six weeks. It would mean my living away from home during the week and coming home on weekends."

I felt my stomach roil and thought I was going to be sick. God was finally pinning me down. I would have to face this thing or just keep on running. The image of Jessica's face sprang into my mind and I made my choice.

"You'll have to go," I said quietly. "And I'll have to stay here with Jess. Alone."

The months before Dan's departure sped by, and my anxiety mounted with each passing day. My family knew of my decision to stay alone, and they were encouraging and praying for me. But as I thought of being alone with Jessica, I tried to shove away the memory of a call that had come in the middle of the night a year after my attack. The voice had been chillingly familiar, as the man on the other end had told me he planned to come back and finish what he had started with me.

Police had put patrols on our house for a few weeks, but as far as I knew, my attacker was still a free man and still knew where I lived. However, the time had finally come for me to free myself from the fears that tormented me.

The day Dan left for school I wanted desperately to stay wrapped in the safety of his embrace, but I unwound myself from his arms and reached down to pick up my child. She had been my motivation for this step of faith and, in spite of my fear of Dan's leaving, I felt strangely grateful.

With a last kiss, Dan was gone. The sound of his engine receded into the distance. The house seemed disturbingly quiet as I put Jessica down for a nap and settled myself into a living room chair facing the front door. I had barely kicked off my shoes when the phone rang.

I hesitated. Was I being stalked? Did my attacker know Dan had just pulled out of the driveway? My breath froze in my lungs as the phone rang a second time.

I grabbed the receiver and answered, my voice barely a whisper.

"Shelly, is that you?"

The voice was familiar, and I let my breath out slowly.

"This is Larry. I really need to apologize to you. I've been meaning to call you for weeks and just haven't been able to find the right moment."

Larry was a friend of ours and a member of the local police department.

"I hope I haven't caught you at an inconvenient time, but I thought you'd want to know the guy who attacked you got sent to prison a couple of months ago. He'll serve at least seven years. I know it doesn't change what happened to you, but I thought it might help you to know he's not out there right now."

It seemed like a lifetime before I was able to speak.

"No, Larry, this is just the right moment. And it does change things. A lot of things."

Mostly, it changed my heart. It showed me God honors our small steps of faith. It showed me, in spite of our hurts and our fears, He can overwhelm us with His love and faithfulness. He had assured me of His presence just when I needed it most.

At that moment I was overwhelmed by God's timing and even His sense of humor. I laughed quietly to myself as I hung up the phone.

My friend Larry's last name is Miracle.

Eagle's Note

by Rita E. Billbe as told by Cheryl Taylor

FLIPPIN, ARIZONA

Lupus took its toll on my body, leaving me chronically exhausted. It produced major conflicts for my career choices, too. After much soul-searching, I decided to pursue my doctorate in music education. But it wasn't long before the strain of the work load accompanied by family pressures, high medical bills, twins attending college, and a husband unhappy with his job, gave me pause. Eventually my health concerns and waning interest in the doctorate had me reconsidering my decision.

I spent hours in prayer looking for answers. Should I drop the university classes and instead obtain my certificate for International Board Certified Lactation Consultant? As the co-founder of an educational Web site for a well-known California pediatrician, I possessed the interest and certainly the knowledge. Many hours spent online assisting women with their breast-feeding questions would count toward the certificate. I could finish the remaining hours required locally. But what about my dreams of teaching at the university level? I continued to beg God for answers to my questions.

The same week I remembered a promise to meet friends for lunch at a local buffet. I didn't want to go. Try as I might, however, I couldn't think of a graceful way to miss the date. Arriving early, I gathered numerous high chairs around a table. Someone tapped me on the shoulder. "Aren't you Mrs. Taylor who taught at Northwest?" a husky voice with a West Indian lilt said.

I turned to see Mrs. Lay, a fellow teacher from the last high school in which I taught vocal music. Our paths hadn't crossed since 1997, but now, in those few minutes, we caught up on our lives. I mentioned my daughter's birth after Mrs. Lay's departure from Northwest. The quiet woman described her new job assignment as an assistant principal for one of the toughest high schools on the south side of town.

Then my friends arrived, and she left to join her daughters. Our conversation centered on child-rearing trials. We regaled each other with the latest antics of our children and time passed quickly. My indecision over a career returned to my mind, and I poured out my worries and fears to my friends.

"I've prayed for an answer, but can't seem to get one. Maybe I need to concentrate more on trying to quiet myself so I can hear His voice."

Someone touched my arm and I turned. Mrs. Lay stood near the table. She said, "I need to tell you something before I go. When we were at Northwest, you put a card in my box with an eagle on it and a verse: 'They that wait upon the Lord shall renew their strength . . .'" I joined in at this point. "'They shall mount up with wings as eagles.'" We both nodded as we finished the verse.

The assistant principal continued. "Through two moves I've kept it and periodically pull it out to read. You wrote . . . 'I don't know what you're going through, and I don't need to, but I wanted you to know I'm praying for you.' I was going through a very difficult time—my husband and I separated. Since then we have divorced and everything is okay now. But you were right. I was really struggling at that time, and your note meant so much to me. I just wanted to say thank you."

As the woman left, I turned back to the table. By this time tears streamed down my face.

One of my friends softly said, "I think you're quiet enough."

Mrs. Lay had just confirmed in my spirit I was a good listener to God's messages, even though my ability to heed Him wasn't confirmed until the present. I hadn't failed to hear God's voice. I simply didn't like what I heard. I needed to make major changes in my life and be open to new paths.

When I could finally convey this in words to my friends, they all began to speak at once. "I could have never made it through those first few months with my new baby without you. You gave me confidence. I knew I had you to turn to." Each line of encouragement triggered more praise around the table.

Suddenly God's answer was evident and I knew the choice He wanted me to make. I attended a lunch date against my better judgment. I bumped into someone who quoted my favorite Scripture and learned what a difference I'd made in the lives of those around me. God didn't send a burning bush in the desert, just a calm West Indian and the wings of an eagle.

Why Now, Lord?

by Kriss Erickson
EVERETT, WASHINGTON

I'd managed to hide the damage of my abusive childhood during my adult life. I believed if I focused on Jesus' example of sacrifice, the darkness of my past wouldn't hinder me. Yet I'd chosen to spend the first thirty-eight years of my life covered by a carefully constructed facade I maintained by brute strength.

When the grief of the first eighteen years of my life broke through my carefully maintained demeanor on the weekend of my church's women's retreat, I learned God held another image of me and would help me choose a new life direction.

Our women's group had planned our annual retreat for months. We'd rented a retreat center beside a peaceful lake in beautiful woodlands near Olympia, Washington. The retreats were a time of spiritual and physical refreshment and reconnection we looked forward to all year.

I was in charge of worship that weekend. Other than the usual last-minute sound equipment challenges, setup went smoothly. As I handed out worship schedules, I felt a sharp pain between my eyes, deep in my head.

I expected it to subside as the retreat progressed. Instead, the pain grew sharper, spreading to my shoulders. The back of my head felt like it was about to explode. Others noticed my distress and showed concern. I was concerned, too. Was I getting sick? But after taking a few deep breaths and saying a silent prayer, I realized my unfamiliar pain was emotional.

As images of my father's angry face and my mother's cold rejection flashed through my mind, I knew I was finally mourning the childhood I'd never had. During this retreat, in this place of peace and reflection, I felt safe enough to loosen the reins making my life appear perfect, allowing my pent-up grief to surface.

That evening I sequestered myself in an unused bedroom to work through the debilitating emotional pain. Images I'd blocked for years—my father's violent beatings, my mother's verbal and emotional abuse—filled my mind. Like the seemingly endless pain of my past, I didn't know how long the hurtful memories would continue.

I'd known, though my parents appeared to be Christians, their treatment of me deserved another definition—abuse. Now the reality of the fear and shame of each blow and every cutting remark pierced my heart. My choice to cover the dark memories now seemed foolish. Without my "everything's okay" veneer, I felt utterly alone.

But I wasn't alone. As He had so many times in my childhood, God made himself known. As the warmth of His Presence mingled with my heartbreaking flashbacks, I hoped He'd make the dark memories fade.

I should've known better. God has shown me since childhood that His is a presence of truth, not a presence of denial. Instead of relieving my pain, His presence helped me endure the current of blocked memories coursing through my mind most of the night. As my most gifted Teacher, He showed me the way to serve Him wasn't by denying my abusive childhood memories, but by looking to Him through them.

Though I tried to be patient with His healing process, I chafed at the fact that I was missing most of the retreat. For a moment I saw my thoughts as if I were observing someone else. This perspective helped me understand I'd chosen to hide my past because I believed my life had value only if I was serving others. Could it be God considered me valuable enough to give me time for healing, even if it meant missing the retreat?

The following day I wandered alone in the woods. I changed direction whenever I felt the Spirit's nudging. At first I felt afraid. I wasn't only shirking my worship duties, but I was using this time for my own healing instead of for the good of the group. But gradually I relaxed. I allowed the peace of the scenery to flow into the ragged valleys of my newly exposed childhood.

Is this what I've forgotten? I wondered as I walked. To follow where God leads? I'd thought I'd chosen well when I left my dark, abusive home and built my life around service. I'd accomplished things my parents said I couldn't do.

"Lord, I was so happy in the way I was serving you," I prayed. "Why did you open me up to pain?"

I felt like the Old Testament's Job, when God asked him to consider Who really ran the world. Could it be possible my Lord was asking me not to deny my painful memories and instead serve Him with all of who I was? Could I really serve Him through my past?

For most of my adult life, I'd been running. I thought I'd run well. But my life turned 180 degrees when the Lord showed me running *from* something was a whole lot different than running *to* something. The retreat turned out to be much more than an anticipated event. The Lord used the time as a way to change my direction—turning me around so I faced Him.

After I led music for the last worship service of the retreat, a friend commented, "I've never seen you so refreshed and open! I really felt God's presence in the service."

As I thanked her, I realized that when I emerged from my walk in the woods, I'd begun a new direction in my Christian walk. Instead of using His salvation to deny my past, I was moving forward by bringing all of myself to Him. My life would never be the same, and for that gift I will be eternally grateful.

God Used Baby Booties

by Venice Correll Kichura

SOUTH WINDSOR, CONNECTICUT

It was a cold and dreary Friday afternoon, only two weeks before Christmas, and I was in the middle of the annual holiday panic. Driving home from work, I was fighting the urge to take a nap when I got home, while my mind sorted out all I still had to do before Christmas.

Thankful the mail carrier had come before I pulled the car into the garage, I stopped at the mailbox, gathering a handful of envelopes, most of them holiday cards, and remembered that I still hadn't mailed out my own cards yet.

Tossing the mail onto the kitchen table, I sorted through them while feeding the dog, defrosting a roast, and making my husband's sack lunch for tomorrow. Suddenly I noticed one of the envelopes was from the twenty-eight-year-old younger daughter of a best friend I had in Florida.

Why would Carrie send me a Christmas card? I hadn't heard from her mom in almost six months, and it seemed like I was always the one initiating a phone call. Since we'd moved away from her five years ago, she'd grown progressively distant as the years went by.

Opening it up, I noted it wasn't a Christmas card at all, but an invitation to a surprise baby shower for Carrie's sister, Mary, my friend's older daughter.

Now I knew we had really grown apart! The friend who used to call me twice a day and pray over everything doesn't even share with me her daughter is married and expecting a baby?

Why did they invite me? They know I can't drive from Connecticut to Florida for a baby shower. These people just want a gift, I mused. I was hurt again. Do they think I can get a gift off in time for a shower a week from today? And right in the crunch of the Christmas season—the busiest time of the year. The nerve of them!

Then, calming down after dinner, my mind switched gears. Without having time to reconsider, I logged onto my computer and did a Google search for patterns of crocheted baby booties. I had only been crocheting for a year and never attempted booties, but I always wanted to do something beyond the basic double crocheted baby blanket, which would take too long to finish, anyway.

I printed out some Internet patterns, sat down with my crochet hook and some yarn, and to my surprise, had two pairs of booties and a matching cap ready to mail out by the end of the weekend. I felt good about it and was actually proud of my first attempt with baby booties. I also had to admit it felt good to have swallowed my pride and done the right thing.

Now I had started a new obsession. Besides cross-stitch, knitting, and needlepoint, I wanted to learn how to make baby clothes!

I wrapped my new, soft creations in some Christmas wrapping paper, scribbled a handmade note, and sent it to my friend's married daughter's address, hopefully in time for the shower next week. I still felt awkward sending them to my friend when we hadn't touched base for so long.

By the time Christmas Eve rolled around, I'd almost forgotten about the booties. Then the phone rang, and it was my old friend, the soon-to-be grandmother. She was so touched by the booties she was bawling.

I soon learned her daughter was not married. This was probably why she stopped calling me, feeling I would be judgmental. In seconds we were bonded back together, even though we lived thirteen hundred miles apart.

Today her new grandson is thriving, and so is our friendship. We're praying with each other again. What's more, I've added a matching baby blanket to the original booties and have even learned to crochet baby clothes. Most of all, I'm thankful God wouldn't let my pride sever a close friendship beginning more than two decades ago.

And to think, I owe it all to an unexpected shower invitation and two pairs of baby booties.

choosing life

You have made known to me the path of life; you
will fill me with joy in your presence, with
eternal pleasures at your right hand.

—Psalm 16:11

Generally speaking, women know and understand the path of life in
a way men can't. For many of us, that first flutter of life inside opens
up a new realm and a chance to anticipate the wonder of a new
living, breathing person emerging from our own body. But choosing
life is so much more than just physically giving birth. Sometimes it
means choosing a path of life for our own existence, conquering
adversity and tragedy to live another day walking in the light of life.
Choosing life is God's plan, no matter the situation. May you be
filled with joy at the possibilities.

Living the Passionate Life!

by Connie Pombo

MARIETTA, PENNSYLVANIA

On March 7, 1996, as I was coming home from work late, I pulled off to the side of the road, laid my head on the steering wheel, and sobbed. "Lord, I can't keep going on like this. You have to do something." I gave God an ultimatum. There was a gnawing emptiness that couldn't be filled with a wonderful husband, great kids, or a beautiful home.

Two weeks later I was waiting for biopsy results from the surgeon's office. My patience had worn thin, so I called to get the results. A cheery receptionist quickly put me on hold while I listened to music. Finally a voice I recognized answered—it was the surgeon.

"Connie, I have your biopsy results." There was a painful silence and then the words tumbled out. "You have breast cancer."

I was in shock. I couldn't believe this was happening to me. Drowning in panic and fear, I screamed the words, "What did I do wrong?" It came from a deep, dark place inside me, a place I kept secret from the world—until now.

I was forty years old. Our boys were just nine and fourteen. They needed a mother. What would they do if something happened to me? I tried to imagine what their life would be like without me—it was too awful to bear.

The following weeks were a blur of tests, more biopsies, second opinions, then finally surgery, treatment, and radiation. Working in the medical field full time, I knew too much. So in an effort to alleviate my anxiety, I would leave on my forty-five-minute lunch break and repeat the words, "Can't be late to radiate. Gotta go, gotta go, gotta go!" Upon arrival at the hospital, I would announce myself by saying, "Excuse me, do you have my tanning bed ready?"

There's absolutely nothing funny about having cancer, but humor was how I coped with my painful illness. On the last day of treatment, I was confronted with the truth about the survival rate for someone with breast cancer. Suddenly I was facing my own mortality for the very first time.

I don't remember walking outside to the hospital parking lot, how I drove home that night, or even how the dozen pink celebratory roses made it to the kitchen table, but I do remember the next few days found me numb. Depression had replaced fear.

In an effort to get me "better," my husband sent me off to California to visit my folks. I will never forget their expression as I stepped off the plane—I was a mere skeleton with a zombie-like gaze, shuffling through the crowd of passengers. They tried to make small talk on the way home, but then they too fell silent.

I spent the following week staring out the window of the guest bedroom. One afternoon Dad came in and sat on the edge of the bed. He had tears streaming down his cheeks as he choked out the words, "Connie, your mom and I have been praying for you, but we don't know what else to do. Please tell us what to do."

"Dad, I don't know what to do—only God can help me now." Without hesitation Dad said, "No, I'm not going to let you do this to yourself. You have to get better—do you hear me? Mark needs you, the boys need you, and we need you. You have to get better. You can choose life!"

Choosing Life

Dad was an expert mechanic. He could take a beat-up old Chevy and make it run like new again, but he couldn't fix me. As a little girl, I would run to him with my scraped knees and he would lovingly put a Band-Aid on it and say, "You're fine, now—go play!" But there wasn't a Band-Aid large enough for this wound.

Seven days later, in quiet desperation, my parents sent me back on a plane bound for Pennsylvania. The good news: I got a seat in a row all by myself on the airplane. I crawled into a fetal-like position and rocked back and forth for six hours.

Arriving back in Pennsylvania I was met by my husband of twenty years. He was expecting to see the all-new Connie—the one my dad had fixed. But she was nowhere to be found.

As we drove up the driveway to our home, I noticed the backyard had been perfectly landscaped. There were colorful flower beds where mounds of dirt had been. The lawn was immaculately groomed, and in the center was a beautiful pink dogwood tree.

"What's this?" I asked, pointing to the tree.

"This is our tree of life—a new beginning. We're starting a new chapter in our lives. Our faith journey begins here. God hasn't brought us this far just to leave us."

For the very first time in weeks, I saw a glimmer of hope. It was brief—but it was there. Up until that time, everything had been in shades of gray, but this was a Technicolor moment. I wanted to hold on to it forever.

The next few weeks allowed me to build on that glimmer of hope. It was between God and me—my husband couldn't help me and my dad couldn't fix me. One afternoon as I looked out at the beautiful pink dogwood tree in full bloom, I asked myself, *What if they told me I had a year to live—what would I do differently?*

I randomly wrote down twenty-seven things I wanted to do before I died. This would become my passionate to-do list. I wrote such things as: spend more time with family and friends, take a vacation to Maine, write a book, take a photography course, and number twenty-seven, parachute out of an airplane.

I laid the list on the kitchen table and Mark picked it up and read each one out loud. Afterward he announced, "I'm going to help you accomplish every one of your goals, and when this list is finished we'll write another one and another one—for the rest of your life."

That was almost ten years ago. I have accomplished everything on my passionate to-do list—except parachuting out of an airplane (I reserve the right to decline)! Facing my own mortality allowed me to ask myself the difficult questions about life and death, but more important it led me on a journey to find out what I was truly passionate about.

On that moonless night on a country back road facing a Dead End sign, my life took an abrupt U-turn. I didn't realize at the time that the Lord did answer my prayer, just not *exactly* in the way that I had expected. It took a life-threatening illness for me to realize what I was truly passionate about, and to carve out an entirely new life. That gnawing sense of emptiness was replaced with a passionate joy for living—God was once again first place in my life.

I believe God allows U-turns in our lives for a purpose. Mine came in the form of cancer. It allowed me to face my own mortality for the very first time and set me on a journey to find out what I was truly passionate about. Now I have the privilege of sharing with others how they too can "Live the Passionate Life"—my most requested retreat topic as a speaker. It all started with the question: *What if I had only a year to live—what would I do differently?*

Do I think my reservoir of passionate to-do's will ever be full? I certainly hope not. In fact, I'm depending on it not to be.

Dying for a Crown

by Sharon L. Fawcett

PETITCODIAC, NEW BRUNSWICK, CANADA

I could sense the frustration in the young doctor's stern voice. "You look like a prisoner in a Nazi death camp! You are starving, Sharon. You have to start eating." Dr. Fenton had been assigned to my case while doing her residency in psychiatry. I was one of her first anorexic patients.

I developed the eating disorder, anorexia nervosa, two months into my first hospitalization for major clinical depression. Having grown up believing I was fat, it pleased me to be losing weight so easily. *This is the one good thing to come out of this miserable experience,* I thought.

I believed I had the illness under control and planned to return to eating normally once I was thin enough. But anorexics live in a world where normal is not possible, lies become truth, and reality is ignored. This is a place where flesh is fat and bone is beautiful. There is no such thing as "thin enough." Giving in to physical needs is weakness; wasting and withering are signs of strength.

My anorexia was partially a response to living an existence that always seemed frighteningly out of control. With my depression, life had become *completely* unmanageable. My body became my kingdom, the only thing I could rule. The treasures of the land were hollow cheeks and stick legs. My crown was made of bones.

Although I was a believer in Christ and knew God loved me, I always sensed I was, in some way, flawed, substandard, inferior. I desperately tried to hide this "truth" from others. By carefully controlling my behavior, my performance, and even my emotions, I believed I might be able to control what others thought about me. I didn't understand God's depth of love for me just as I was.

I worked very hard and managed to make people believe I was a bright, talented, decent person. The more praise I received, the better I felt about myself. I began gauging my value by my achievements and deeds.

I burned out at the age of twenty-six. Exhausted, I no longer had the energy to do anything. I couldn't concentrate on the simplest of tasks and lost interest in all the activities I had previously enjoyed. I withdrew from others, just wanting to be alone, quiet, and still. I had everything to live for—a loving husband and two beautiful daughters—but I began to long for death. I felt like a failure as a mother and a wife.

My first admission to the psychiatric ward came just days after my baby, Jenna's, first birthday. As the door to the unit closed behind me, I thought, *What is someone like me doing in a place like this?* I felt defeated and confused. My days of achieving had ended; my greatest accomplishments became getting showered and dressed in the morning.

My need to succeed at *something,* and my lifelong dissatisfaction with my body, made me vulnerable to anorexia nervosa. The quest for thinness became my new focus in life, something to fill the void, and I worked hard at it. My thoughts became consumed with calories, my weight, and ways to avoid eating. As I reached weight-loss goals I had set for myself, I was still dissatisfied with my appearance. "Just five more pounds" became my mantra.

The illness progressed and I became increasingly weak. While someone else cared for my children, I slept eighteen hours a day.

I grew battle-weary. I longed for a normal life and knew my first step would have to be to give up the quest for "thin enough." I resolved to start eating healthy meals again, but soon discovered it would not be easy.

I always felt terribly guilty, defeated, and angry with myself after I ate. One evening after finishing a meal, I was leaving the hospital dining room when I heard a hideous voice inside my head. Full of loathing, it screamed at me, *You fat pig! Why did you eat that? You've ruined everything!* I had never heard anything like it before. It was very frightening. My doctor knew I was struggling, but I never told her about the enemy in my head.

The harder I worked to get well, the more vocal the hateful being became. *No, no, no* was all I could hear. I felt like two people in one body, one who wanted to live and another who wanted me dead. I realized I was no longer in control. Someone, or something, had seized my throne and it appeared I was now at its mercy. Each day I became weaker. I tried to eat but often was too tired to even chew.

One afternoon, after realizing I would not live much longer as an anorexic, I found myself looking through my closet for something to wear to my own funeral. I was ready for death—but I was not willing to leave a legacy of pain and torment behind for my husband and children. I knew I had to live for them.

After three years of battling my psychiatrist, I resigned myself to trusting her to tell me how much to weigh and what to eat—no matter what the voices shrieked. In this way I managed to overcome the eating disorder, but the depression remained.

I tried everything the doctor ordered, hoping each new treatment or medication would be the one setting me free. But the depression would always sink its claws deeper into my soul, drawing me away from the edge of the pit, back into the darkness.

As my husband parented our children, I focused on trying to stay alive. I had many hospitalizations during the next six years and my absence was difficult for my family. My eldest daughter, Lauren, asked, "When will you be coming home *forever?*"

After a total of nine years, twenty different medications, two hundred electro-convulsive treatments, and eighty weeks of hospitalization, I realized if I was ever going to find a cure for my illness, I had to look elsewhere. While home from the hospital, I chose to see a Christian counselor.

Berys was unlike any counselor or therapist I had ever spoken to. "I don't have all the answers," she said, "but the Lord does. He can replace all the no's in your life with yes's!" Through prayer she invited Him into the counseling process, and it was prayer that started my journey toward healing. It was prayer that turned me toward a new direction. Berys also taught me how to listen for God's voice and study His Word.

The angry, condemning voice was replaced by God's loving, tender one, speaking softly to my wounded soul. As I listened, I understood the roots of my depression reached to the core of my spirit and my entire life had been based on a lie.

I had worked so hard to hide my inferiority, but I was not the worthless person I had always believed I was! I was the handiwork of the Creator of the universe, created in God's image, a beloved child of the King.

"Yes, my daughter, I love you, I will not forsake you," He said gently to my wounded soul.

I began to discover it was not a number on a scale determining my value. My achievements did not matter. My lineage or who I was did not determine my worth—*Whose* I was did. I belonged to God.

God told me He had a plan for my life, a future full of hope. He said, "You will seek me and find me when you seek me with all your heart . . . and [I] will bring you back from captivity" (Jeremiah 29:13–14). He fulfilled His promise. Within three months of my initial meeting with Berys, the depression was gone. I never had another electro-convulsive treatment. I never returned to the psychiatric ward. I no longer needed medication or the care of a psychiatrist. Five and a half years have passed and I remain free from depression and from anorexia nervosa.

For my daughters, my husband, and me, it has been a wonderful "forever."

I spent thirty-five years looking for fulfillment and value in all the wrong places. My quest almost killed me, but God used it to transform me, to turn my life around. Finding my true identity was the key to unlocking the heavy door to the dungeon I had been imprisoned in for nearly a decade. I have learned peace and contentment cannot be found in work or wealth, or even weight. By discovering the God-given worth, inherent in us all, I was lifted out of the dark pit of depression to stand in the glorious light of His love. God took my crown of bones and replaced it with a crown of life.

Was Blind But Now I See

by Marie Golden Partain
STARR, SOUTH CAROLINA

On a bright, Indian-summer day in 1995, I went to have a routine mammogram. The technician was a beautiful young redhead who had worked for my ex-husband, Wendell, several years before and had become an X-ray technologist working for the radiology clinic. While she was preparing me for the torture of this cruel test, we casually discussed my least favorite subject, my divorce from Wendell. This did, however, keep me from thinking about the imminent pain I would have to endure. I admired her proficiency and professionalism.

As she completed each view of my more than ample breasts, she developed the film and returned for other views. Her smile faded and our chatter became more forced. She made every effort to avoid alarming me. As the strain for both of us became greater and her eyes no longer hid her emotions, I finally said, "Terri, don't forget I used to work oncology. I know something is wrong. Let's just get this over."

Her eyes brimming with sadness, she said, "Dr. Warren will see you next door."

As I entered his office, the films stared ominously from their perch. "Is that it?" I asked as I viewed what might be my harbinger of death. Having worked for a prominent oncologist, I had seen this numerous times. Dr. Warren asked whom I wanted for the biopsy and called to schedule it as soon as possible. I left his office frightened and overwhelmed, but a biopsy was scheduled for the next day.

By Labor Day I was recovering from a mastectomy without complications and had begun to accept my altered body image.

The words of Doris Lessing, "Coincidences are God's way of remaining anonymous," chimed in my head. My reconciliation with Wendell over the prior several months became clear. What I would have done without either God or Wendell I cannot imagine.

During my recovery, the prayers and visits of friends with whom I had lost touch blessed me. Relationships with eight of my oldest and dearest friends were rekindled. We began seeing each other as often as we could.

Marsha, a member of our group, was diagnosed with breast cancer several months later. I had been very fortunate to have a pencil-eraser sized, encapsulated, non-aggressive lesion; Marsha was less fortunate. Her malignancy was advanced and very aggressive. She endured chemotherapy and bone-marrow transplants. No human being could have fought more diligently than she did. *The Girls*, as we dubbed ourselves, were always there for support and encouragement.

Marsha and I spent countless hours together sharing our hopes, fears, and dreams. The purchase of her first prosthesis, we did together. On this same day Marsha found this beautiful palazzo pantsuit she encouraged me to buy. In fact, she said, "Marie, this is so you! If you aren't buying it, I am buying it for you!" Marsha loved gorgeous, flamboyant clothes. I am much more conservative; but to humor her, I bought the outfit having no idea when or where I would wear it.

It was not unusual for Marsha and me to be at Dr. Malik's office on the same day for our appointments. She was always decked out with color-coordinated clothes, shoes, hats, and jewelry. She had several wigs, each styled differently, and she was stunning in all of them. In fact, she was beautiful with her bald head shining, but she seldom allowed anyone to see her that way.

One evening The Girls met at Applebee's for dinner. Three of us arrived early. I noticed Marsha was pale and perspiring. She leaned toward me and said, "Get me out of here. This wig is making me too hot." I put my arm around her as she had her first seizure. She was able to regain composure and swore us to secrecy about the incident. She continued treatment and never lost her positive attitude.

Shortly thereafter, she came to my house to help me hang pictures. Not only was she meticulous about her wardrobe, but she could dress a house with the same flair. She grasped every opportunity to use her talents and energy wisely. While we were hanging pictures, she casually asked, "When are you and Wendell remarrying?"

I laughed and told her, "His only stipulation is we marry on July twenty-ninth so he won't have to remember another anniversary date. Since that is only two months away, it probably won't be until next year."

This was one of the only times she ever let me know she was uncertain she was going to beat this cancer. She said, "I want to help with your wedding, and I'm not sure I'll be here next year."

Two months later, on Monday evening, July 29, 1996, Wendell and I had a small wedding at our church. Marsha helped decorate for the reception given by The Girls. She made the tablecloths, cut magnolia leaves and ivy to decorate the social hall, and made a beautiful watermelon fruit basket. She brought all her serving dishes and made her own Swedish meatballs.

Although she had not been fond of Wendell when we eloped in 1965, she was now one of Wendell's most avid allies. She knew he had to love me to support me through breast cancer. She also appreciated his encouragement of her husband. Only she and I understood what a tremendous burden cancer puts on spouses.

Marsha continued to struggle and fought her cancer with all she had. On her last visit to Dr. Malik's office, her son carried her in his arms to the examining room. Several days later, she was admitted to the hospital and never returned home.

On a Saturday night I stayed with her to give her family a night of rest. She asked, "Marie, am I going to die?" I had promised her I would always tell her the truth, but the words affirming the inevitable almost choked me.

The only response I could make was, "What do you think?"

She just smiled and asked, "Do you see Jesus over the door?" I nodded yes and she drifted off to sleep.

A few days later, as I was taking my break with a friend at work, I felt a warm breeze touch my face. It felt as soft and sweet as a good-bye kiss. I immediately told my friend to let our supervisor know I was going to the hospital. When the door opened to the oncology unit, Marsha's husband hugged me and said she had died about fifteen minutes before I arrived (just enough time to drive from work). I am sure Marsha kissed my cheek as she left this earth.

The family asked The Girls to sit with them at the funeral. We were all devastated. It was hard to believe her fight was over. We were all tearful and somber until Elvis Presley's "Peace in the Valley" wafted through the chapel air. Nobody but Marsha would have Elvis sing at her funeral. We knew this was inspired by our friend to lessen our grief and give us peace. The Girls looked at each other and began to laugh hysterically. I am certain the mourners filling the chapel thought we were crazy, but we knew Marsha was right there laughing with us.

At the cemetery we sang "Amazing Grace." I could hear the voices of The Girls as we sang this beautiful song while we said our good-byes to Marsha. As the words from the first verse said, "I once was lost but now am found, was blind but now I see," I was enlightened.

After Marsha's death, my irritability and restlessness became more intense. I questioned God and myself. Why was I spared when she wanted so desperately to live? It was only after one of my psychiatric patients was diagnosed with breast cancer that I began to find my purpose. God gave me the opportunity to expend all my energy reuniting her with her estranged family and supporting them through their grief process.

I recognized God had a plan for me, and I was led to take the lay speaker certification classes offered by the United Methodist Church. The first time I spoke at our home church, Marsha was right there with me. I wore the flamboyant palazzo pantsuit she had insisted I buy. From my jam box, Christy Lane, in an upbeat song, belted the words, "I want to give something back to this world before I go." I knew this was what I wanted to do.

Although I remain uncertain of why I was left and Marsha went to be with God, I found my purpose. I have chosen to use my talents whenever I have the opportunity and to use my energy wisely, just as she so often did. I no longer feel guilty I survived, but I have a genuine desire to give back just a little of what has been given to me. It's a choice that has changed my life, and I thank God—and my dear friend Marsha—for helping me to make it.

When Love Held My Hand

by Jaye Lewis

When I heard the heavy steel door clang shut, it was a comforting sound. Somehow I felt nothing could touch me now. My entire world had come crashing down; yet in the quiet of the psychiatric ward, quite unexpectedly, I felt safe. Terror stalked outside the door, but inside it could not reach me. I was certain God had abandoned me.

My relationship with God had always come easily, and now He seemed so far away. It was almost impossible to see or hear Him, when my eyes and mind and heart were filled with confusion. I was very angry with God at what had befallen me, and I railed at Him. I prayed in hopeless anguish. How could this happen? Why did He not protect me? Where was God when I needed Him so desperately? Why was He not with me in my darkest hour?

Sometime during my first morning in the psychiatric ward, my pastor visited me. I was surprised and touched he had come so quickly. Surely he would have some words of comfort for me.

"Pastor, I don't know if I believe in God!" I sobbed. He sat like a rod of iron, his eyes averted, his face stiff and unyielding.

"Perhaps if you confessed your sin, then you'd receive an answer as to why you are in this place," he barked, giving me a look of disgust. I felt as though I'd been slapped. I just sat there looking at him, wondering why he had bothered to come at all.

"You must be very busy," I said coldly. "Perhaps you'd better go." My eyes followed him as he stood up. I thought his face looked

God Allows U-Turns for Women   154

awfully unhappy. He hesitated, looking more lost than I felt.

"Well . . . if you need anything . . ." Without meeting my eyes, he handed me his card.

"Sure," I said with bitter sarcasm, "just in case I want someone to confess to." I took the card and watched him go.

Tears spilled from my eyes and ran down my cheeks. Lifting my feet into my chair, I hugged my knees and buried my face. I felt forgotten and shunned. Later I walked slowly to the nurses' station and handed the nurse his card. I told her to place his name on the list of people I never wanted to see. I was certain now God had forgotten me.

The next morning I was interrupted in my ceramics class—one of the many activities the experts believe will make a patient feel normal while in an institutional environment. Someone to see me? At ten-thirty in the morning? Who could it be? Believe me, when you wind up in a psychiatric ward, it's highly unlikely you're going to send out invitations! There were very few people who even knew I was in the hospital, so this visitor was a complete mystery.

I walked out into the lounge, anxiously looking around. Sitting by himself at a table across the room was a tiny elderly man. As soon as he saw me his face beamed. Hesitantly, I smiled back. He beckoned, and I looked around, making sure there was no one else whom he might be expecting. Why would he come to see me?

I walked over, knowing this must be a mistake. He must be here to see some other patient, or perhaps he too was a patient. He stood up and held out his hand. It was a small, frail hand, but his handshake was surprisingly firm. He squeezed my hand with both of his.

Choosing Life

It was a warm feeling. Reluctantly, I slipped my hands away as he began to speak.

"I'm a traveling pastor, and someone told me you needed me."

"Who told you?" I asked, shivering.

"That's not important now," he said with a smile, "but *you* are important." He again reached out and took my hands in both of his. He radiated such warmth that his blue-veined hands were almost hot to the touch.

"How can I help you?" he asked, his voice filled with compassion.

All of a sudden my eyes welled up with tears and I burst forth with my story. He listened, and the expression on his face mirrored my every emotion. When I cried, his eyes filled. When I laughed, he chuckled. When my face contorted with grief and anguish, his face nearly broke with sorrow.

"Oh, Pastor!" I cried. "I don't know if God loves me! I don't know if He knows I'm alive! I don't know if I even believe in Him!" The pain poured out of me like a flood. I waited for that look of disgust, but all I saw was love. This man loved me, and he didn't even know me! At my outburst, he smiled into my eyes.

"My dear," he said, "if you can't believe in God right now, then maybe it will help you to know that I do." Warmth flooded through me. At that moment I was certain I was in the presence of unconditional love. Smiling, he pressed my hands. Then he turned and walked toward the big steel door. In the doorway, he turned again, still smiling.

"God be with you," he said softly. The door clanged shut behind him, but strange as it seems, I felt as though he had left a part of himself behind.

It was a long road back to healing, but I made it out of the hospital and back into a restored life. Many years later, I'm still amazed to discover what a precious gift my nervous breakdown was. It taught me I can hold a hand and give comfort to a stranger. It taught me I can touch a heart with just a few words. It taught me I can love without condition. It taught me I can laugh and cry and never be ashamed. It taught me God is as close as my next heartbeat, and when I least expect Him, He will always show up.

I have walked through many a dark valley since the day love held my hand, yet I have learned as long as I choose to trust in God, I will never walk alone. I chose life during a dark time, and at long last the sun is shining and I know God's rainbow of promise is for me.

Living in the Faith Zone

by Betty J. Johnson
PARKER, COLORADO

I received my first sledgehammer blow when the surgeon walked into the waiting room and said, "I'm sorry, Mrs. Johnson. The tumor is inoperable. The cancer has spread to all parts of Richard's body."

This must be a nightmare, I thought, trying desperately to comprehend what this man in green scrubs was saying.

"We just returned from an Alaskan cruise," I stammered, trying to fight my way out of the nightmare into reality. "Just look at him. He's a big, robust, healthy-looking guy."

"Be thankful you took that trip when you did," the doctor responded.

"Are you trying to tell me we won't be taking more trips?" I asked.

"I'm sorry. There was nothing I could do." He sighed.

"If you're trying to tell me there is no hope, I won't accept that," I whispered. "We're Christians, and that means there is always hope."

During those next weeks, our family, friends, and especially I walked down a path of hope, believing and expecting a miracle. Not only did I expect a miracle, I did all in my power to make it happen. Day and night I cared for my husband of forty-six years, my high school sweetheart, and my best friend. "I can do all things through Christ who strengthens me" was my stronghold. Each day I claimed this Scripture over and over. I could not, nor would not, accept the fact that Richard was dying. If I could find the right doctor, pray hard enough, say the right words, selflessly care for him, I was convinced we would receive our miracle and he would go into remission.

Then, at 5:30 A.M. on January 21, 2003, I finally got the message—I'm not the Big Controller. When the doctor awakened me and led me from the hospital room, saying, "Richard's heart has stopped and he's not breathing," I felt completely out of control. What was I going to do? How could I live without my soul mate? What happened to our well-planned life? My road of hope was gone. I was on a dead-end street—without Richard—all by myself.

Actually, in the recesses of my mind I knew God was somewhere. But where? I didn't understand why God had allowed this horrible thing to happen, but I knew, no matter how miserable I was, I would be more miserable without Him. Somehow, someway, my faith in God had to be my new path. Not that I hadn't been on this path before, but this time I knew who was in control. The Bible verse, "For we walk by faith, not by sight" (2 Corinthians 5:7), led me as I put one foot in front of the other, one minute at a time.

One night I picked up a book prodding me to trust in God. While reading, I laid the book down and cried out, "Where are you, God, where are you?" Suddenly a card dropped out of the book, and the words on the card seeped through the walls of my broken heart.

It was a poem reminding us that our loved ones who had gone before us were happily waiting for us in heaven, bathed in His everlasting light. We only needed to be patient, and our time would come to be reunited.

The message reassured me Richard was safely home. He was not

Choosing Life

alone and I was not alone. I sobbed and snuggled into my newfound faith zone.

Two days later a friend called and suggested I contact another new widow. "Teri's going through the same grieving process," she said. I called Teri and found someone who understood—another reminder I was not alone.

"Shall we call Bob and the three of us get together next week?" Teri suggested. "You know his wife, Betty, died just four days before my husband, Jack."

Bob and Betty and Richard and I had been in the same Bible Study group for the previous three years. I felt comfortable meeting with Bob and Teri, and we began weekly meetings, forming a life-saving and life-changing grief support group.

"I'm so tired of people asking, 'How are you doing?' when I can't tell them what I'm feeling," Teri commented.

"Sometimes honesty is not the best policy," Bob answered.

The tears flowed, honest feelings erupted, dependency on each other increased, and our special bond strengthened. Before Bob left for his summer vacation with family and friends, he announced, "You girls saved my life this past year."

"I believe God brought us together and we saved each other," Teri responded.

"It looks like He's in control," I commented.

When Bob returned in the fall, he, Teri and I met for an update on what was happening in our lives.

"I'm responding to God's nudge," Teri said. "I start my classes in divinity school next week. The strange thing is, this is not something I would've done if Jack were still living. I still miss him, but I'm excited about becoming a pastor. It gives me a glimmer of hope for my future."

"You know, I bought a new RV before I left here last spring," Bob remarked. "I've decided the two main hobbies I'd like to pursue—besides visiting my family—are traveling and golf, but I just don't enjoy doing either by myself."

"I can relate," I answered. "I feel like I'm living in a 'couples' world' and I don't fit in. I've tried playing golf with our old group of friends and joining them in their social outings, but these experiences usually just remind me of how much I miss Richard and how much my life has changed. Thank God for my children and grandchildren. They're my connection to the past and my hope for the future."

One unusually warm winter day, Bob called. "How about joining me for nine holes of golf?" he asked. "I'm tired of playing by myself."

For the first time, we shared laughter as well as tears.

During the next months, because of Teri's class schedule, Bob and I often met without her. Sometimes we'd walk around the nearby lake, talking about the continuing changes in our lives and how we were coping with a lifestyle that neither of us had ever wanted.

As Thanksgiving approached and everyone focused on being thankful, a close friend asked me, "Remember what I told you months ago? You had a rare marriage, one many people never experience for even one year, yet you had forty-six years. Since it's Thanksgiving, can you be thankful now?"

Her words were God-sent and God-timed. As I began focusing

on being thankful, I tiptoed into the acceptance stage of my grieving process.

"I'm tired of this lifestyle. How about let's start having some fun," Bob suggested later that month. "Like going out for dinner tonight," he offered—and I accepted.

Our dinner conversation began a gentle U-turn in both of our lives. Bob suggested we start practicing what we were preaching—"treasuring the moment."

"I'm not sure I know how to have fun anymore," I answered. Then, as though the words were coming from someone else's mouth, I heard myself say, "Let's put our future in God's hands."

"I can't think of a better place," Bob answered.

The next months found us spending more time together. We still grieved, but now we laughed more and even giggled at times.

"It's as though God knows what we need before we do," Bob often said. "This is a road I never planned to travel," he'd add.

Nor had I. Even though Richard had often told me he wanted me to go on "living life to the fullest," I turned a deaf ear to those comments, knowing I would never enjoy life again, let alone find someone to treasure the moments with. We continued to pray our way through the "dating" process. *Bob is God's gift to me—and a test,* I decided. Worrying about others' opinions had been a way of life for me, and now I lived in the faith zone, trusting God to lead the way.

Not only did He lead the way, He prepared the way as our children, grandchildren, and friends all opened their hearts to our good news—we would always love Richard and Betty; however, we discovered that our hearts had room for another love. Living in the faith zone resulted in our marriage. Sometimes I still grab the control wheel. Then I remember the trauma, the pain, and that horrible out-of-control feeling, and I let go and trust in God. I readily admit we don't know what path our future will take; however, Bob and I do know, no matter where we are physically, we're going to keep trusting God, and that means we'll be living in the faith zone.

Precious Emma

ROLLA, MISSOURI

My career of choice has always been motherhood. Managing our home and farm, being involved in church, PTA, and 4-H is just where I wanted to be.

With three healthy and happy children already, no one could understand my need for another. I took these thoughts and my desires to the Lord in prayer over and over and was always comforted by the feeling that in His time, I would have another child.

But time was running out. I'd been challenged with endometriosis and uterine infections since adolescence. Having children had not been easy. I had never taken for granted that God had blessed me with my family.

My doctors said it was time to quit trying, I needed a hysterectomy. Yet I chose to wait three and a half more years before conceding to schedule the surgery. The day I had the routine pre-operative blood work and tests done, I cried all the way home from the doctor's office.

On the way home I prayed God would either give me the strength to accept the fact I was not going to have another child, or let me know in no uncertain terms I should not go through with this.

Just a few hours later God came through loud and clear. The doctor's office called to tell me that when they tried to schedule my surgery with the hospital, a nurse identifying herself as Joy said the requested day was out of the question. The entire week was already booked for elective surgery. When the nurse asked me what I wanted to do, I told her I would have to get back with her. I knew in my heart God did not want me to have the surgery.

Two weeks later, on the very day I was to have had surgery, I learned I was pregnant! When I called the doctor's office to let them know, the nurse told me a very surprising story.

"I think you've got a guardian angel! I called the hospital to schedule a C-section the same day I talked to you, and they swore up and down there wasn't anyone named Joy working there. Weird, isn't it?"

At the time I had the pre-operative blood work done it was still too early to detect the pregnancy. Had I not asked for God's wisdom and guidance, our precious Emma would have ceased to live, and we would never have her wonderful presence in our lives. God chose life for my daughter, and I praise Him daily for that gift.

Emma is six years old now, and while I love all four of my children dearly, I cannot look at Emma without being reminded of what we would have missed out on had I not chosen to allow God to turn me in the right direction.

Lessons From Monterey Street

by Cheryl Haggard
STAR, IDAHO

Caroline Augusta Gildemeister Schwander Lorensen looked out from a cheap dime-store frame. From the top of her freshly permed, snow-white hair to her perfectly polished patent-leather pumps, she emulated a woman rewarded for her weekly walks to the corner beauty shop. Her seasoned smile caused her worn eyelids to camouflage the piercing baby blues the German heritage could only call their own. A meticulously lacquered cane rested gently on her chair, an indication her age and stubborn nature weren't going to keep her from walking gracefully through the sunset of her life. Her gnarled, age-worn hands rested quietly in her lap, as they took a much-deserved respite from the mouth-watering chocolate fudge and mulled cranberry sauce she made at Christmastime. She had a reason to smile that day: The photographer caught the essence of a woman who had just turned 102 years old.

My brother and I visited Great-Grandma at her two-bedroom house on Monterey Street, the home she had occupied for over eighty years. She greeted us with her infectious smile, goldfish crackers, and ginger ale. After exchanging pleasantries, Great-Grandma escorted us to her sticky, plastic-covered davenport where we begrudgingly listened to her tales of times past—stories we had heard more than once, as if history really did repeat itself.

Then, the gentle scolding began for having my bangs in my face: "Good German girls should never hide their blue eyes" (even though mine are hazel). And when I brought my first college beau to her for approval, she pointed a plump finger at me and said, "He's not the one."

A later boyfriend gave her reason to give me the twinkle-in-her-eye confirmation I was eagerly anticipating. Holding my face in her wieldy hands and with a giddy look on her face, she said "Now, he's the one." Great-Grandma was right: we've been married for almost fourteen years.

After the stories, snacks, and scolding, she would grab her over-sized King James Bible and recount what God had taught her that week. She pointed out Scriptures that corrected and comforted her. She pulled out notes she had painstakingly written with her arthritic hands, and tenderly shared the treasures in God's Word. We then retreated to her piano where she played the hymns of old. Our favorite was "How Great Thou Art." Although we sang off key and off beat, we made a joyful noise on Monterey Street.

Saying "Auf Wiedersehen" began with a trip to the garage for canned goods and eventually ended with twenty minutes of blowing kisses as we drove away from a piece of living history. As a child, I left Great-Grandma's house stuffed with goldfish crackers, ginger ale, and canned peaches. As an adult, I have come to realize I was filled with much, much more.

I recently studied the picture on my dresser of my great-grandmother and wondered how she could look so happy at age 102, after all she had been through. My mind raced back to the dreaded news I had just received from my children's doctor: My one-and-a-half-year-old daughter, Molly, had the same disease as my three-year-old son, Caleb. They have a rare immune disorder that will render them ill most of their lives. They have accumulated a collection of ear tube surgeries, adenoidectomies, tonsillectomies, and CTs of their sinuses. They have been prescribed gallons of antibiotics, steroids, and pain-killers. The most difficult prescription is the monthly intravenous blood infusions they must endure.

As I recounted what we had gone through and will continue to go through, my thoughts shifted from my pain to Great-Grandma's. How did she survive the grief of outliving two husbands, losing the first in the early years of marriage with babies crying at her feet? How did she cope with outliving two of her three children: one a victim of war, the other of cancer? How did she handle the sting of racism, being called a Kraut as her family sought safety in a German refugee camp in Canada? Then I smiled; how did she survive any of this without disposable diapers, fast food, or a microwave?! The only answers to my questions and comfort I gleaned was her smile captured so eloquently in the picture, years before.

A few months later I returned home from a long day at the hospital. It was Molly's day at the "city" and my mom's turn at caring for our two boys left happily behind. Hospital days are hard, no matter how well I prepare myself. Coming home was just as difficult as I returned to the "reality" of homework, housework, and the Crockpot.

As I sifted through the goodies my mom customarily brought me—articles from my hometown newspaper, coupons, and hand-me-down magazines—something out of the ordinary caught my eye. The mysterious object became more familiar to me and for a moment, I forgot how to breathe. My fingers gently inspected the edges of the weathered binding of the book as if I was touching my firstborn for the very first time. Mom presented me with Great-

Grandma's Bible, and unbeknownst to both of us, she had just handed life back to me.

I began to leaf through the worn pages as if I was eating a piece of her fudge, looking for anything to ease the pain of my day; my life with sick children. Great-Grandma often clipped out comic strips, Ann Landers' advice, or quips from magazines that would inspire her, then tucked them in her Bible for safekeeping. *There must be something she clipped out here for me!* I thought to myself. *C'mon, Grandma! You lived for those bits and pieces of paper . . . where are they?* I found a few tidbits, but nothing that satisfied what ached inside of me. As I sat on my bed, frustrated with my treasure hunt, God began to work at my weary heart. Like the gentleman He is, God whispered to me, "Grandma didn't find comfort in the words of this world, but in My Word." That was all He needed to say.

I began to retrace my thought pattern and looked at her Bible with new vision. I studied the magnified words carefully underscored, page after page of passages that meant something to her. Some even evoked memories of her sticky davenport, goldfish crackers, and ginger ale on Monterey Street. I read the notes she had hand-written in the margins, as if I was reading someone's personal diary. I felt as if I were trespassing onto the pages of history. Her private history. Then I got it. Grandma chose life through God. It was her unyielding faith that saw her through those difficult times. Her Bible is where she found comfort and answers to life's toughest questions. This is how she made it. This is why she smiled. And this was how I was going to gracefully handle life's most difficult curve balls. And maybe, just maybe, I too will be smiling at 102.

Waiting at the Crossroads

by Sharen Watson

HIGHLANDS RANCH, COLORADO

The words of Solomon's song flowed over, around, and through me. *"Arise, my darling, my beautiful one. . . ."* It was a familiar passage, but never so relevant until that very moment. The song went on to describe the passing of my spiritual season. *"See! The winter is past; the rains are over and gone."* Music filled the sanctuary, and His Word touched my spirit. I tilted my head upward with expectation and rose in anticipation. My waiting was over. He was moving me. *"Arise, my darling, my beautiful one, and come with me."*

The previous two years had been a time of waiting, searching, listening, and watching. Contentment had been hard to find, and I ran circles trying to find fulfillment. "Is this what you want me to do, Lord? Do you want me to give more time to the schools, to the church? I'll do it all. I'll do it all for you. Just tell me; I'll do it!"

I was tired—no, I was exhausted. "Do and do" was my motto. And then, literally, I was bedridden. A virus kept me in bed for two long months. I was undone and all my works ceased.

Recuperation was slow at best, and I found myself standing at the crossroads of my life. "Where do I begin again, Lord?"

And He showed me.

In a quiet moment, He revealed my place. My journal lay open in my lap and I put my pen to the page. Simply, I drew a cross. I worshiped Him for His sacrifice, His amazing love. Knowing we weren't finished yet, I closed my eyes and waited. *What else, Lord?* Again, my pen went to work. Listening to the still, small voice of

God Allows U-Turns for Women

my Savior, I drew dashed lines within the boundaries of the cross. Crossroads.

"Where do I go, Lord? What direction do I take?" I stared at the representation in front of me. I placed a small dot, representing my presence in the middle of the cross. "Here I am, Lord."

Stop. Stay right where you are. Those were the words impressed on my spirit. The words were not audible to my ears, yet firm in direction, and I had a choice to make. I could make my own pathway and keep walking, or be still at the center of the cross, symbolically closest to the heart of our crucified and risen Savior—unmoving. I chose God's way.

Content in the crossroads for the next few months, I spent my time caring for my family at home and seeking God without the distractions of *do*ing.

Only one thing required my weekly attendance: ladies' Bible study. Worship was my soul focus. Surrendered to my Father, I was empty of myself. And then, in the quietness of reflection, He decided to sing over me through His Word. And my waiting was over.

With surrender came His commitments. Not manufactured of myself and not decided by pressure or coercion. His path was before me. The crossroad was a place of rest and growth, but when it was time to move, He did the leading. A new ministry was birthed, but my hands are open. It's His, not mine. No longer the frenzy of "do and do," the Christian writers' group I lead is built on His foundation. I merely serve. And He leads me still.

"My lover spoke and said to me, 'Arise, my darling, my beautiful one, come with me'" (Song of Solomon 2:10).

choosing salvation

"Who are you?" he asked. "I am your servant Ruth," she said. "Spread the corner of your garment over me, since you are a kinsman-redeemer." —Ruth 3:9

Ruth asked for Boaz's covering, but what she really wanted was the salvation he could bring her, by redeeming her from a life of widowhood and aloneness. It sounds sad in this day and age, but back then widowhood could also mean starvation and defenselessness. And without Jesus as our kinsman-redeemer, we starve our spirits and stay defenseless against the world, our fleshly desires, and wiles of the evil one. Choosing to let Jesus wrap us in His garments of grace and mercy brings us the protection and spiritual nourishment as well as comfort and peace we long for. And we don't even have to tell Him who we are. He already knows and is waiting for us. He longs to cover you in His love. Will you let Him?

The Bride

by Carol Genengels
SEABECK, WASHINGTON

"Boy, I've really done it this time," I muttered. "How do I get myself into such predicaments?" I stared at the pathetic creature sprawled in the back of my husband's pickup truck. What a mess.

Lifeless eyes stared from a face smudged with dirt, and someone had drawn a crude mustache above her lips. Her scarlet fingernails were chipped and broken. Her lopsided wig and clothing reeked of stale cigarette smoke.

My husband rolled his eyes and quipped, "I can't believe you sent me to a tavern to get her. You should have heard the guys when I carried her from that dive. What have you got up your sleeve this time?"

"Think what you spared me from, honey," I said as he walked toward the house.

The problem started when our Christian women's group agreed to decorate a meeting hall for an upcoming spring retreat. The theme was to be The Bride of Christ. Our committee envisioned a beautiful bride awaiting her bridegroom. There was one small problem: we needed a mannequin. Since we had a very limited budget for the task, we hoped to borrow one.

I scoured department stores and thrift shops to no avail. No one could help us out. Mannequins are very fragile and expensive; it seemed doubtful anyone would loan us one.

A friend suggested calling ABC Rentals, and when I called, the man informed me they didn't carry mannequins.

"Can you think of anyone who might have one?" I begged.

"Sorry, lady."

"Thanks anyway."

"Hey, wait a minute!" he said. "I just thought of something. There's a tavern down in Old Town—they have a mannequin . . . dressed in a sailor suit. Maybe they'd let you borrow her—or something, it's worth a try!"

"Er, sure, thanks."

I hung up the receiver and decided I'd better pray. "A tavern, Lord? Should I get a mannequin from a tavern?"

I summoned my courage, took a deep breath, and dialed the number.

A woman's voice answered. "Old Town Tavern."

"Uh . . . hi . . . my name is Carol, and I've got a problem."

Silence.

"I'm in charge of decorations for a women's retreat, and we really need a mannequin to model a wedding gown."

"Yeah?"

"I've been trying to find a mannequin all over town, but I'm not having much luck. I called ABC Rentals, and a guy there said you have a mannequin in your tavern."

"Sure do!"

"I was wondering if we could possibly rent her for a weekend. I realize mannequins are very expensive—I promise we would take very good care of her."

Hearty laughter resounded. "I'm sure you wouldn't treat her any worse than she gets treated around here . . . that poor ol' gal could use a retreat."

"You mean it, we can borrow her?"

"Well, I gotta warn you, she's kind of a mess. The guys—you know. But she should clean up with some soap and water."

I thanked the lady and made arrangements to get the mannequin a few days before the retreat. That's when I cajoled my husband into picking her up for me.

When I saw the dirty mannequin in the back of the truck, I suddenly felt very weary.

I lifted my precious cargo from the vehicle and gingerly carried her into the house. I carefully placed her on a sheet and removed her wig. I filled the bathroom sink with liquid soap and dropped the crusty wig into the bubbles. The water turned the color of weak black coffee. Next I removed her blue denim bell-bottoms and tossed them into the washer. I felt sickened by what I saw. Her lower torso was covered with obscene graffiti. I got a pail of clean, soapy water and began scrubbing away the scars of depravity. I gently washed her face, dissolving the mustache, and bathed her arms and upper torso. Her sooty gray skin became a soft peachy color. I felt great joy bubbling up within me as her original beauty surfaced.

I began to talk to the Lord. "Where is this joy coming from?"

He gently answered, "That's the joy I feel when I wash away sin, and the beauty of my original creation emerges."

I felt energized as I continued my task. I soaked the wig two more times before it no longer left a sooty trail in the basin. Soft, shiny curls formed as it dried.

I dressed the mannequin in underwear and a full crinoline underskirt. Next I slipped my daughter's floor-length wedding gown over the bride. The billowy white gown with three tiers of embroidered ruffles seemed tailor-made. Again the Lord spoke to me: "I have a robe for my bride that fits perfectly and is without spot or wrinkle."

As I pinned a floor-length tulle veil to her silky hair, I was aware of just how still and yielding she was to my touch. *I wish it were this easy with all of them,* I imagined the Lord to say.

The weekend of the retreat everyone admired the beautiful bride standing on the stage in front of dark blue velvet curtains. Baskets of lilacs and mock orange blossoms graced her sides, and she held a bouquet in her white-gloved hands. No one would have guessed her humble home.

I shared her story of cleansing and invited them to make a major choice in their lives and become part of the bride of Christ.

"Perhaps some of you have graffiti on your body or soul you'd like washed away." The response was amazing.

When the ladies learned of her circumstances, many were saddened to think that she had to return to the tavern. The Lord reminded me of His grief when the redeemed return to a sinful environment.

A few days later I returned the sparkling mannequin. She was dressed in a clean T-shirt and bell bottoms. I gave the proprietor a thank-you note and said, "You'll never know what a blessing this mannequin was."

"Hey, she looks a lot better. Were you able to clean off all of the graffiti?"

"Yes," I said, "it all came off."

"Thank God!" she said.

"Yes," I agreed. "Thank God."

From New Age Spirituality to the Foot of the Cross

by Pamela V. Norton
WETUMPKA, ALABAMA

Things are going pretty well. I took a sip of my gin and tonic, and took in the view of the Rogue River. *So why do I feel so uneasy?* I fought against the disquiet in my mind, trying to shake the uncomfortable feeling creeping into my seemingly wonderful life.

My husband walked toward me carrying his third gin and tonic, and we dangled our feet off our new, well-outfitted, eighteen-foot raft. Drinks in hand, we discussed the details of our upcoming fishing trip to Alaska, and for the moment, the uneasiness disappeared.

Later that evening my husband and I joined our friends. All of us were in our early to mid-fifties, and our conversation seemed to hover around personal retirement and the stock market. Two of our friends had retired the year before and were traveling through Europe, while we rafted through the Rogue's protected "Wild and Scenic" section, wishing we were them. But in the back of my mind, I couldn't help but notice that we were complaining when we should have been enjoying our experience on the river. It was a passing thought, but a thought unusual for me.

Several months later it was time for my yearly "birth chart" reading. Everyone knew I consulted the best tarot card reader and astrologer in the Pacific Northwest, and most of her clients were business professionals like myself.

"Pam, you're about to enter a new level of contentment in your life," she said as she slapped down the tarot card. It all fit, the "birth chart" reading and the tarot card predictions. The only problem was that she only had a track record of being right less than half the time.

No, something is wrong . . . very wrong. That same uneasiness I'd felt on the river enveloped me again. I walked slowly down the steep stairs from my psychic's office to my car. I was shaken and couldn't make out why.

It was the beginning of 2001, and while driving through the back hills of Eugene, I thought of Jesus. *Could He possibly be who He claimed to be?* I laughed, pushing the ridiculous thought away. I had tried the Christian way of living, but turned my back on God and the church years before. Not even my good friends knew that I had gone to a Bible college, had been a pastor's wife, and served in the ministry in my twenties. I didn't tell many people about my "religious" background because they would probably struggle believing it. I was the woman who had arrived at her "higher self" through meditation, crystals, astrology, positive thinking, hypnotherapy, spiritual enlightenment, and inner-child work. That was my foundation—religion wasn't.

That year my life changed quickly and radically. By the time 9/11 transformed the world, I was divorced and living in the South again. With a résumé boasting several successful business start-ups, along with marketing and public relations job experience, I couldn't figure out why I was struggling to find a job.

Nothing I tried worked out. I lived off my savings account for a year, and then the money ran out. Late notices started filling my mailbox. I was confused. There had always been ups and downs where business was concerned, but I never had trouble manipulating success back into my life.

During that time I met and married my husband. Between my patient mother and supportive husband, I felt a fate worse than drowning in my bills. They had stepped in to care for me. But as I reflected through my self-pity, thoughts of God filled my mind again.

Is it possible that the Bible is really a long letter from God to us, His creation? Is it true that Jesus is really the Son of God, and that everyone needs salvation that only He can offer?

This time I didn't push my musings away. I sat down in my living room and pondered them. I also thought of my daughter and her husband and the loving Christian home they were providing for their children—my grandchildren. I knew my mother and sisters had been praying for me since I turned my back on the Lord almost twenty-three years earlier. And I remembered the person I had been when I first became a Christian in my late teens. Finally I thought about Jesus, who had taught the greatest lessons of love I had ever heard; His willingness to turn himself over to the authorities of His time, to be brutally beaten and painfully nailed to the cross. *Jesus, who quietly looked down on a jeering crowd, including me, and asked God for our forgiveness.*

In that moment, I dropped to the floor and surrendered my life to God. It had taken a long time, but it happened that quickly. I prayed for forgiveness for the horrible acts committed through my life of greed, self-centeredness, and decadence. For days I was in constant prayer, remembering all the things I'd done against God and the standards He set for us through His Word.

I was nothing. I had nothing to offer when I made my U-turn and fell before Him that March morning in 2002. I struggled until there was no struggle left. Ego, pride, independent nature—they were all gone.

The point of surrender was my second chance to find healing, and once again to be set free from the emptiness of a life full of materialism and the betrayal of the New Age spirituality I had so blindly accepted. I made my choice, the choice to submit to God. A U-turn choice that changed my life.

It has been three years since my return to the foot of the cross, and God has restored my relationship with my children I had left so long ago when I went off in search of "personal fulfillment." I have a close relationship with four grandchildren who love the Lord, and they love their grandmother. I am the member of an evangelical church whose members have a heart for the lost. They are teaching me to put on the armor of God, to walk in His protection and love.

Occasionally they ask me if I miss the lifestyle I lived in Oregon. I tell them it holds no temptation for me. There is a song that comes to mind, a song that tells me I have been rescued, and now, the world holds absolutely nothing for me.

I am amazed to think of God's grace and forgiveness in taking such an arrogant child, who claimed to have arrived at "God consciousness," through my "higher self." I continue asking God to keep me on my knees, never allowing me to stray again. I never want to be away from my Lord and Redeemer again.

As Psalm 40:2 reads, "He lifted me out of the slimy pit, out of the mud and mire; he set my feet on a rock and gave me a firm place to stand."

Choosing Salvation

The Lemonade Stand

by Gayle Zinda
STOUGHTON, WISCONSIN

What am I doing here? I wondered as I pulled up to an ordinary office complex, not quite sure why I'd come or what I expected. It was nothing exciting—concrete, glass, a few trimmed shrubs and dwarf trees. *Odd place for a restaurant,* I thought as I snooped around. I was looking for something called The Lemonade Stand.

I spotted a large carved wooden sign—a pitcher of lemonade. Below the sign, on the glass, were the words *Wigs, Breast Prostheses, and Makeup. Okay, not a restaurant.* I went in . . . and stepped through my own looking glass.

The sterile office complex gave way to a plush Victorian parlor. In the center was an antique salon chair. There, one woman was literally transforming another. I watched as the lady in the chair went from bald, pale, and self-conscious to smiling, radiant, and confident—all with a little wig work, some makeup, and a few kind words.

I was a nurse administrator for a group of Ob/Gyn doctors. We delivered babies. Happy things with happy people, it was a sunny world. But I knew what breast prosthesis meant—the dark side of medicine—cancer.

Yet this parlor was anything but dark. It was a little slice of heaven, warm and inviting. And the woman who left the chair glowed as if she had been reborn.

I was here because a saleswoman had slipped me a note. Our medical supplier said to me, "You gotta meet this woman." *Yeah, sure,* I thought. *I'll call her right away.* I dropped her note into my purse and forgot about it.

For a year.

One day, during a moment of quiet between patients, I remembered the note and thought, *Why not?* So I called, and this nice lady answered and said, "Honey, I've been waiting for your call."

You've been what? Waiting for my call? You don't even know me! I thought.

She said something about my being the answer to her prayers. Then there was something about Jesus. So she invited me down to meet her. Before I knew what I was doing, I said, "Okay, when's a good time?"

Now I was there and she was heading right for me. She was dressed sharp and done up nice, just like it was Saturday night—or Sunday morning, if you prefer. She was on the lighter side of forty and looked feminine and radiant. I thought to myself, *If she looks that good, why is she walking with a cane?*

"Honey, I'm Rita," she said. "I'm dying and I know it, but the good Lord told me if I hung on long enough, He'd send someone to carry on this business. As soon as you walked in, I knew it was you."

We had known each other for ten seconds, and this lady was telling me it was God's will I take over her business. *Is she kidding? God's will?*

I thought I was a good person—after all, I was raised Catholic. I wasn't perfect, but I tried to do the right thing, be nice and polite. *Be kind to crazy people!* But I simply wasn't used to people saying

"God said" this or that—certainly not about me. I smiled weakly at her.

I wasn't job hunting. I was happy where I was. It was positive, life-affirming work, making people happy. I had the respect and friendship of my colleagues. My position paid a great salary and had tremendous benefits.

I was a success. Although . . . sometimes it didn't feel like it.

Sometimes I felt like I was spinning my wheels and going nowhere. For all of the salary my position paid, I wasn't taking much home. My divorce a few years before left me with mountains of debt. I had two school-aged boys, Adam and Nicholas, to raise on my own. While my parents were a big help, and my boys were supportive, hard-working angels, the long hours at work had me worried I wasn't spending enough time with them. In darker moments, I wondered if I was doing anything right.

As Rita told me her story, my problems paled in comparison. She was diagnosed with cancer at thirty-six. During the years of chemotherapy following, she lost her hair nine times—including her eyebrows.

Chemotherapy makes life difficult for cancer cells. Unfortunately, this makes it hard on other cells, too. Some people get sicker than they have ever been or totally exhausted. Their skin and lips dry up. To top it off, their hair falls out. You don't *look* like you anymore. You don't *feel* like you. I imagined the looks of pity, even fear, you'd get from others.

You want to be treated normally, so you try to put yourself together again. But you're so tired, wiped out. You need proper prosthetics and lingerie. You need special cosmetics. You've never seen a wig before, and now you need a good one. The department store salespeople give you the pity look, or even worse, show you indifference—you're just another receipt. And the next thing you need is always somewhere else, far away. It is exhausting, humiliating, and profoundly demoralizing.

That is what Rita suffered and what she decided to change. She created The Lemonade Stand to bring it all together, to revive and refresh other patients. She put them back together on the outside and rebuilt their spirit on the inside. She did it all, even as she suffered with them.

Now her time was running short. *Makes my problems seem pretty small,* I realized. The amazing part was she wasn't bitter or angry. There was fire in her eyes, and Rita glowed from within as she told me I could help these people, too. It wasn't like the room got brighter or anything, but you could feel the certainty rolling off her in waves. I asked myself, *How can she be so positive?*

The idea of helping these people was attractive—almost enough to get me to change jobs. But it was her sense of purpose, her drive—strangely combined with a powerful serenity—that pushed me over the top. *I want to feel like that, too.*

Divine inspiration, talking to God—this was a new way of looking at life. Even with my upbringing, it seemed a bit improbable. Then she took my hands in hers and asked, "Have you ever asked Jesus to come into your heart?"

The hair on my neck stood up, but not from some heavenly spirit; it was more a *Wow, this is weird!* kind of feeling. *Ask Jesus into my heart, huh?* I bit my tongue and tried not to grin as I thought about it. Rita waited patiently for my answer, a corner of her mouth turned up in a smile. She saw right through me. Sheepishly, I said, "I'm not sure what you mean."

"Just that, honey," Rita grinned. "Ask Jesus to forgive you for your sins and come into your heart, from this day on." While my logical mind was still whirling, my heart knew I needed to do this, and I made the choice at that moment to ask Jesus into my heart. We said a prayer and, at her prompting, I asked. I felt odd and guarded, but I certainly was sincere.

"There, honey. Now you don't have to worry anymore." She patted my arm. "Now Jesus will send you the help you need, and in return He wants you to help the people He sends to you."

A few simple words, an open mind, and I was in. No heavenly light, no choir of angels, and no *I was blind and now I see*. It just kind of grew on me. Doubt, confusion, even fear remained, but over the months ahead they withered and died. Calm and certainty grew and blossomed within.

I gave up the security of my former job and jumped into the unknown. I learned to do a thousand things I'd never done. But every day began with a Bible verse. "Nothing else matters," Rita said. "All the skills in the world won't help if your heart's not in the right place. If we get that right, the rest takes care of itself." Philippians 4:13, "I can do all things through Christ who strengthens me," became my favorite verse.

Rita was so right.

The Lemonade Stand grew to three locations and helped over ten thousand patients regain their strength and spirit. Many returned as volunteers. Others took up the cause: scores of donors, uncounted relatives, dozens of professionals. They gave of themselves to keep Rita's vision alive.

One of those professionals became my husband, Michael, and my family was whole again.

There were never great financial rewards, so some might say it was less than successful. But I know ten thousand and more who would argue otherwise.

More important, now I no longer ask, *What am I doing here?* God made a choice to send His Son to die for me. I made a choice to accept Him as my Savior, and then I made a choice to help others. Two choices changed my life—two choices I will never regret.

His Reflection

by Janet Eckles
ORLANDO, FLORIDA

Out of habit, I felt for the light switch in our bathroom. I flipped it on, but the darkness remained. My body shook with terror. Holding on to the cold, slick counter top, I looked toward the mirror and saw a dreary gray of nothing. In desperation, I felt the urge to scratch through the glass into the darkness to find even a slight glimpse of my reflection . . . instead, I found the ugliness of my black world.

Blindness entered my life with a vicious force, ripping apart the dreams my husband, Gene, and I had. Our focus was on raising our three sons and living the "happily ever after." But the unavoidable effects of a retinal disease, with no possible cure, turned our joy to bitterness and fear.

Motivated by desperation, I began a relentless search for a cure. My visits to fortune-tellers, psychics, and New Age healers caused my bank account to diminish and my frustration to increase. My despair touched those around me.

"How are you doing?" a friend asked one day during a phone call.

"Fine," I lied. The old Jan, with a cheerful personality, had vanished.

"Well, I don't know how you feel about attending, but our church is having a service you might like," began my friend's invitation. Before I could give her a quick excuse, she added, "Actually, it's a Bible study followed by prayers for healing."

There was my answer—the place where I'd receive the miracle.

"I'll go with you!" I replied, and caught myself smiling, something rare for me those days. I knew I would be one of those lucky people and be healed. I welcomed this invitation as a much-needed intermission for the wrestling match of my emotions.

But instead, this experience left me full of disappointment. The services proved worthless. No healing. No miracle.

"Why, God?" I asked over and over again.

While attending the services, my eyes poured out tears and my mind, irrational thoughts. Chances were, everyone present at these sessions was burdened by some degree of personal problems, but I reasoned none could be as bad as mine. I resented all those who attended. Unlike me, all were sighted and were able to jump in their cars and carry on with their lives. They could all see and were more than capable to resolve whatever their issues were. But what chance did I have to move forward?

My heart became much like the metal folding chair I sat on: cold, hard, and lifeless. But in a subtle and unexpected way, the first breath of life entered my soul. It stopped the pounding of my heart and, with a mixture of power and gentleness, Matthew 6:33 caused me to pause and look up: "Seek first the Kingdom of God and His righteousness, and all these things shall be added unto you."

A quick sigh slipped from my lips and, momentarily unaware, my sobbing stopped. What I heard entered my heart like a flood-light revealing every detail of the source of my pain—I had been consumed with the desperate desire to see again. This was my number-one priority—nothing else mattered. But God instructed otherwise: to seek Him first.

Seek Him first? But how?

I had a decision to make: I could continue to sink into my sorrow, or I could look up, open my heart, and see what God would do. I chose the latter, accepting Jesus as my Savior, my Lord, and my all. The promise I heard in that verse from Matthew warmed my heart.

The miracle I hoped for was called freedom. Like opening my hand to let go of a helium balloon, I opened my heart and released my pain, bitterness, and sorrow. Although I wasn't sure what the next step would be, I saw the evidence of this transformation back home with my little ones.

"Hey guys," I greeted them, "I'm home. Did you behave for Daddy?" I tossed my purse onto the couch and scooped my three-year-old, Joe, into my arms. "I need a big hug."

"Need some help?" offered Gene.

"Nope, I'm home and I'll take over," I assured him. "Come on all of you, it's bath time." I rounded them up.

Instinctively, I counted the steps down the hallway and felt for the banister to head upstairs.

My hearing had become more acute. With little effort, I could pick up any telltale sound directing me to correct their mischievous behavior.

Gene's tone of voice also revealed his moods to me. One evening he walked into the house and I heard his briefcase plop onto the counter. "I've got a surprise for you," he said in a singsong tone.

"Oh, should I close my eyes?" We both laughed out loud.

I felt a square object in my hands and ran my fingers to examine it. "Cassette tapes?"

"It's a set of cassettes of the Bible," he answered.

I squealed like a little girl as I clutched them to my chest. "It's better than any gift you could give me, better than a huge diamond!" I hugged him long and tight.

The Word of God nourished my soul and placed a permanent light into my darkness. I gained wisdom to see my family with my heart and care for them with my love.

My vision became clear as I recalled the time I anguished, unable to see my reflection on the mirror. But now with new eyes, I perceived a new image—a portrait painted with the splendor of God's love, the vibrant colors of His sustaining power, and delicately framed with the golden reassurance of His promises.

Single

by Maggi Normile

MOON TOWNSHIP, PENNSYLVANIA

In the movie *Jerry Maguire*, the title character, played by Tom Cruise, tells his love interest, "You complete me." In the Britney Spears song, "When I Found You," she sings, "I found myself when I found you." And on television we have one reality show after another in which contestants battle it out to win someone's heart. With views like that penetrating our lives day in and day out, it's no wonder so many people believe that in order to be whole, to feel loved, and to be happy, you need to be in a relationship—and if you're single, then something *must* be wrong with you.

At least, that's what I've been told.

During my teen years, I did what most hormonal raging young girls did—I drooled over cute boys and went out of my way to make myself look good in order to catch their attention. I always had to dress up when leaving the house, and goodness knows it would have been a sin for me to walk out the door without makeup! I flirted. I flaunted. I did all the things young girls think they need to do in order to grab the attention of the male persuasion.

And yet for some reason, I never did get the boyfriend I wanted.

As I entered my twenties, I was still single. My friend Heather was with her first boyfriend, and I'm not afraid to admit I didn't care for the guy. It wasn't because I was jealous, even if that's what she thought. I just didn't understand dating someone who had no problem racking up *your* credit card bill or bragging about getting into fights, as if it made him Mr. Macho.

Over and over again Heather wanted to set me up with one of his friends, and each time I said no thanks. One time she actually told me I needed a boyfriend, and when I still declined her offer, she asked in all seriousness, "But what will you do when people find out you don't have a boyfriend?"

The sarcastic side of me wanted to throw myself down on the ground and pound the pavement, while screaming, "I'll die! I'll just die! My life is over! IT'S ALL OVER!" But I just shrugged my shoulders.

Of course, Heather isn't the first person in my life who's made me feel I needed to have a man on my arm. From the time I entered my twenties until now, as I'm about to enter my thirties, I've had some of the most outlandish comments and questions posed to me:

"You've *never* had a boyfriend? What's wrong with you?"

"You're too picky."

"What are you, gay or something?"

"Nice guys like that don't exist."

"You better find someone soon. You're not getting any younger."

"You need to lower your standards."

"I hope I'm married *and* have kids by the time I'm your age."

Believe it or not, a couple of those comments came from Bible-believing, God-fearing Christians.

Then there are people who assume if you're in your twenties and still haven't dated, it must be because you've never been asked out. After all, nobody could possibly choose to not date! Could they?

The truth is, I have been asked out, but quite frankly, none of those guys was worthy of my time or attention, let alone my

Choosing Salvation

affections. I decided I'm better off waiting for Mr. Right instead of settling for Mr. Right Now.

Yes, I am nearly thirty years old and have made the choice to remain single.

What a concept!

After a while I just became worn out. I was so busy chasing after a relationship and not getting very far, I starting believing something must be wrong with me if I couldn't find a boyfriend. I began to forget who I was. I had lost myself in the midst of believing my identity was wrapped up in whether or not I could capture the attention of some guy. It wasn't until my late twenties I was struck with a revelation: I wasn't still single because something was wrong with me. It was because God was protecting me.

Call it divine intervention if you will, but I firmly believe God kept me from finding the relationship I had always longed for because He knew I was chasing after the wrong things. He knew if He allowed me to have the boyfriend, I very well may have compromised my morals and done things I didn't want to do, all for the sake of being loved and accepted by someone. I was buying in to the lie that my identity was wrapped up in whether or not I could find a man and how much attention he was going to give me.

God obviously knew better than I. He knew what I was capable of, even if at the time I would have said, "Not me. I'd never do anything I didn't want to, just to have a boyfriend." The truth, though, is many young girls and women find themselves in compromising situations without understanding how they ended up there. How many times have you heard someone say, "It just happened"? But it didn't just happen. Many of us get wrapped up in the moment, and we enjoy feeling loved and having so much attention that we don't pay attention to our actions and how they may affect us later on.

I realized I did need a relationship, but I was looking in all the wrong places and at all the wrong people. I needed a relationship with the one person who could fulfill every single one of my desires and give me all I longed for . . . and that one person wasn't some Joe Schmoe down the street.

I had been a Christian since I was sixteen, but it took me ten more years to finally get it into my head that my self-worth wasn't meant to be wrapped up in what some guy thought of me. It was meant to be wrapped up in Jesus Christ and what He thinks of me. It's all about who He is and what He did for me. I was so busy trying to find a man to give my heart to, and daydreaming about finding my one true love, I never realized my true love was right there in front of me the whole time, His arms opened wide, longing for me to turn to Him with all I had to offer.

I finally discovered it's not until we give our entire hearts to Christ and look to Him for what we need and desire, that we truly begin to discover all we are, all we're capable of, and all we can be. He's the only one who can give us our heart's desires. He can give us true happiness lasting a lifetime. But He can't do that until we stop chasing after worldly desires and begin chasing after the One who gives life—and gives it to the fullest.

Sure, a part of me still longs to one day find a knight in shining armor who will sweep me off my feet, but I'm willing to wait. I'm willing to trust Christ with my heart and let Him decide when the time is right for that part of my life to happen. Even if I remain single until I'm sixty, or even if I never marry, then that's okay. The only relationship I need in order to lead a fulfilling life is with the Lord Jesus Christ. He can and will take me places no earthly relationship ever could.

I found myself when I found Christ.

The Doll in the Attic

by Marcia Krugh Leaser

FREMONT, OHIO

When my mother passed away, my sister, brother, and I had the arduous task of going through all of Mother's things and deciding what to keep. Mother was a pack rat. I believe she kept every single thing throughout her entire lifetime.

And if that wasn't bad enough, her mother did the same.

While in the attic, crawling through dust that was eons old, I reached under the floorboards and felt something strange.

My mind imagined a hundred things it could be until, at last, I saw in my hands the most decrepit-looking doll I'd ever seen.

Both arms—with no hands at all—hung by threads. Her hair had long since rotted off, and instead of eyes, empty holes stared back at me. Her clothes were nothing but rags, and she was so terribly dirty her face couldn't be seen. I threw her into a box to be taken downstairs.

Often, throughout the next few weeks, I came upon this ugly doll and was faced with the decision to keep her or throw her away. More than once she was in the "trash" pile, but something always made me drag her out again.

One day as I was sitting amidst all the books, boxes, and bags, I saw her limp, frail body laying on top of a dirty pile of newspapers. I picked her up and nonchalantly began rubbing her face. Layer after layer of dust was removed, and I was amazed to see a white bisque head, red pursed lips, and tiny little teeth. Although she had no eyes, dark eyelashes were painted above and below where the eyes should have been. Beautifully shaped eyebrows arched perfectly on her snow-white forehead. I could tell she had once been an exquisite doll.

Imagine my surprise when I took her to a doll hospital and found, much to my chagrin, she was very valuable. A treasure amid the dust. Her original body was intact, but she needed new arms and legs.

I have no idea to whom she belonged or why she was shoved into that dark, dingy place. I only know how glad I am I didn't judge her the way she first appeared.

I had often prayed for wisdom to better understand my life, and I began to see this doll story as a life metaphor. I too had been lost. My life wasn't what I had wanted it to be. I oftentimes chose to crawl beneath the floorboards of life and hope no one ever found me. But I was found . . . by Jesus Christ.

He didn't look at how I first appeared, either. He saw beyond all the dirt and grime of my life. He cleaned me up, dusted me off, and loved me enough to teach me His saving way of grace.

He saw something valuable in what *I* felt wasn't worth bothering with. I was valuable enough to Him that He went to the cross and died.

Once I chose Him to enter my life, I knew, beyond a shadow of a doubt, if I'd been the only one on earth, lost in an attic, He would still have gone to that cross . . . just for me.

Ever After

by Carolyn Byers Ruch as told by Christina Greene

HATFIELD, PENNSYLVANIA

My life began as a fairy tale. I was a chosen child, adopted from an orphanage when I was just a baby. Now I would know the love of a mother's touch and the protection of a father's love. I was blessed.

But just like the gruesome fairy tales of old, my life took several grim twists between my "once upon a time" and my "happily ever after."

I was just nine years old when I went to spend the summer with my aunt and her family. I made the journey with the anticipation of getting to know my cousins, and I dreamed of having playmates from morning to night.

Playing with my older cousin was fun! He enjoyed showering me with attention and making me giggle with glee, especially when he tickled me. Until one day the tickling wasn't so fun anymore. My giggling ceased. *What is he doing? What's happening? He can't put his hand there, can he?* Feelings of shame and helplessness flooded my mind.

I whimpered over and over, "Please, stop! No. Please. Stop it!"

Finally his selfish exploration ended. My body was free from his controlling grip, but the memories of his touch would never leave my mind. I believed it was my fault. And I no longer believed in fairy tales.

Returning home, I thought I could rest in my parents' care, far away from the awful memory. Yet just three years later another

Choosing Salvation

experience would send me into a state of utter shock.

I was home sick from school.

"Dad, my stomach hurts!"

"Go back to bed. I'll be up to help you in a minute."

The kind of help I expected and deserved never came. The man who was supposed to love me without ever expecting anything in return, the man who promised to be my father—and my protector— became my ultimate betrayer. Rubbing my tummy would have been understandable. I had a stomachache. But fondling other parts of my body in the process was another devastating blow to my fragile soul.

"Mom, make Dad go away. Make him leave!" I burst out one day. "I don't want him to live here anymore."

"What are you talking about?"

I stared up into her emotionless eyes. I felt lost. Alone. How could I explain something for which my twelve-year-old vocabulary had no words?

"This is his home," she continued. "Why should I ask him to leave?"

All I could do was beg, "Mom, please!"

As if my mother somehow knew this day would come, she grabbed my arm and led me to my bedroom. Rummaging behind the dresses, shoes, and toys in my closet, she pulled out dozens of pornographic magazines and stacked them methodically at my feet.

"Is this why you don't want Daddy here anymore?" The tone of her voice was strangely even—almost robotic. "Did you find his collection of trash? Did you think I didn't know about it?"

I was stunned, speechless, and sick to my stomach. I stood there, in my own room, feeling as exploited and exposed as the women on my dad's magazine covers. My mother had no idea what was happening; she thought I wanted him gone because of this filth. I had two choices: numb my mind or become completely unglued. Denial became my closest friend.

My mother didn't offer any tears or explanations, just encouragement to maintain a stiff upper lip, to move on and be strong. After all, that is what she had done her whole life. It is what her mother taught her to do.

My father left us a few months later, and my mother and I began to face our lives together as passive victims to my father's sins.

The symptoms of my abuse affected me during my teen years and on through my years in college. I began searching frantically for something—anything making me feel valuable. This perilous pursuit led me into the arms of men who reaffirmed my belief that my existence was for one purpose only—pleasing them sexually.

Then one winter day I made what I believed to be an unredeemable choice. I had an abortion.

I lay curled up in my bed, sobbing. My body was throbbing, but it didn't even compare to the anguish encompassing my mind. I needed help.

I had withdrawn from my mother months ago. I didn't want to hear another word about the bad choices I was making or about how Jesus could change my life. She had found God and I wasn't interested. Yet now I was alone. I knew I couldn't live one more day . . . not like this. I was desperate. I reached for the phone.

"Mom, I need help." I could barely utter the words—the tightening muscles in my throat restricted each word.

Choosing Salvation

"Christina, honey, what's wrong?"

"I have cramps and . . ." I could not stop the tears. I could hardly catch my breath as I went on to describe my symptoms, which were more emotional than physical, it turned out.

"Honey, did you have an abortion?"

"Yes," I whispered.

I'll never truly know how she knew. Maybe it was her medical background, or maybe it was because mothers just have a way of figuring stuff out.

But I'll forever treasure what my mom shared with me that lonely night.

"Christina, do you still have the Bible I gave you several years ago?"

"I think so. I think it's in a box in my closet with some of my old textbooks."

"I want you to read it, Christina. Start in Romans and then read the gospel of John. Cry out to God, Christina, and ask Him to speak to you. I promise He will. I'll be praying for you, honey. And please see your doctor first thing tomorrow morning. I love you. You're going to be okay. There's nothing you have done that Jesus didn't die for. Nothing!"

I stumbled to the closet and found the cardboard box loaded with several years of college texts. I tossed many to the side until I found it, *The Good News Bible*. I made my way back to the bed and sat down.

"God, help me. Please!"

I found Romans and began to read slowly at first, trying to make sense of it all. Then my eyes landed on words speaking of a love I had never known—a completely selfless love. I understood. Jesus had died for every wrong I had done and for every wrong done to me. I continued on through the gospel of John. I cried tears I had never shed before—cleansing tears. One by one the words began to gently unravel the shame and guilt I had wrapped around my heart. The message was clear—I was loved! No matter what I had done— no matter what I'd become. Jesus loved me and I chose to trust His love. Indescribable warmth surrounded my body. I felt His comfort. And for the first time in my life, I lay in another's arms, fully exposed and unashamed.

This was just the beginning for me. More than thirty years have passed since I was first violated; the abuse I endured remains a part of me. It has left scars, as old injuries do. But I don't allow the story of my past to write the story of my future. I have made a U-turn. I choose to live each day trusting in the words I read that night. When I get discouraged, I have learned there are counselors and loving friends who are quick to listen and slow to speak.

Today I live a life not defined by the moment when I was first violated, but by the moment when I chose to embrace Jesus. The pain of my past cannot compare to the joy I have found. And I am resting in His arms . . . ever after.

CHAPTER eight

choosing love

This is how God showed his love among us: He sent his one and only Son into the world that we might live through him. This is love: not that we loved God, but that he loved us and sent his Son as an atoning sacrifice for our sins. —1 John 4:9-10

God gave us a wonderful gift through His love for us. We, as children of God, have the same capacity for love. Whether it is love between a husband and wife, a parent toward their child, grandparents and grandchildren, or the love of a close friend, we all have the ability to choose love. Yet that choice is not always easy. Choosing to love is the greatest gift we can give to God.

I Am Woman, Hear Me Roar?

by Nancy C. Anderson
HUNTINGTON BEACH, CALIFORNIA

My brother Dan said, "I'm going home. Your bickering is driving me nuts. Your constant fighting's more irritating than chewing on tinfoil!"

I defended our behavior. "Hey, it's not like we disagree about *everything*. Ron and I agree on all the major issues. We hardly ever fight about big stuff like how to spend our money, how to raise Nick, or who's a better driver. Just the little stuff gets to us."

He sighed and said, "Well, I'm sick of hearing you go to war over where to put the towel rack, which TV shows to watch, or who left the lights on. It's all dumb stuff. None of it will matter a year from now. Why did you have to criticize the way he mowed the lawn? I know it wasn't perfect, but couldn't you just let it go?"

"No," I replied. "I don't want our neighborhood thinking of our yard as the ugly one. So I told him to fix it, big deal. We were married in the seventies and Helen Reddy told me I had to roar if I wanted to be heard, so I roar—and it works, because he re-mowed the lawn and I won."

Dan paused, shook his head, and said, "If you keep this up, you may win the arguments but lose your husband."

I smacked him on the arm and said, "Oh, stop being so melodramatic."

The next evening Ron and I went out to dinner with friends we hadn't seen in several years. We remembered Carl as being funny and outgoing, but now he seemed rather sad and looked exhausted.

His wife, Beth, did most of the talking. She told us about her fabulous accomplishments at work, and she endlessly bragged about her brilliant, Mensa-bound children.

She didn't mention her husband, except to criticize him.

After we ordered our dinner, she said, "Carl, I saw you flirting with that waitress." (He wasn't.)

"Caarrrrlll," she whined, "can't you do anything right? You are holding your fork like a little kid." (He was.)

When he mispronounced an item on the dessert menu, his wife said, "No wonder you flunked out of college—you can't read." She laughed so hard, she snorted—but she was the only one laughing.

Carl didn't even respond. He just looked over at us with an empty face and a blank stare. Then he shrugged his sad shoulders and looked away.

The rest of the evening was even more oppressive as she continued to harangue and harass him about almost everything he said or did. I thought, *I wonder if this is how my brother feels when I criticize Ron.*

We said good-bye to Beth and Carl and left the restaurant in silence. When we got into the car, I spoke first. "Do I sound like her?"

Ron meekly said, "You're not *that* bad."

I asked, "How bad am I?"

"Pretty bad," he half whispered.

The next morning, as I poured water into the coffeepot, I looked over at my "Famous Quotes for Wives" calendar. "The wise woman builds her house, but the foolish tears it down with her own hands." *Or with her own mouth*, I thought.

"A nagging wife annoys like a constant dripping." *How did I turn into such a nag?*

"Put a guard over my mouth." *Oh Lord, show me how!*

I carefully spooned the vanilla nut decaf into the pot, as I remembered the day I forgot the filter. The coffee was bitter and full of undrinkable grounds. I had to throw it away.

Then it dawned on me. *The coffee, without filtering, is like my coarse and bitter speech.*

I said, "Oh God, please install a filter between my brain and my mouth. Help me to choose my words carefully and speak in smooth and mellow tones. Thank you for teaching me the 'Lesson of the Coffee Filter.' I won't forget it."

An hour later Ron timidly asked, "What do you think about moving the couch over by the window? We'll be able to see the TV better."

My first thought was to tell him, *That's a dumb idea! The couch will fade if you put it in the sunlight, and besides, you already watch too much TV.*

But instead of my usual hasty reply, I let the coarse thoughts drip through my newly installed filter and smiled as I said, "That might be a good idea; let's try it for a few days and see if we like it. I'll help you move it."

He lifted his end of the sofa in stunned silence. Once we had it in place, he asked with concern, "Are you okay? Do you have a headache?"

I chuckled, "I'm great, honey, never better. Can I get you a cup of coffee?"

Ron and I recently celebrated our twenty-seventh wedding anniversary, and I'm happy to report that my "filter" is still in place—although it occasionally springs a leak. I've also expanded the filter principle beyond my marriage and have found it amazingly useful when I speak to telemarketers, traffic cops, and teenagers. Choosing to love might not be the easiest, but it is always the best option.

It was such a long time ago . . . over twenty-five years. But what choice did I have? I was young, in college, and I saw no way out. I pretended it was an easy decision. I convinced myself there was no other choice. The people at the clinic presented a clinical and impersonal description of the options and made a required—but feeble—attempt to present them all. Their bias was very clear and, at the time, reassuring. After all, it upheld my decision.

The tiny life already established in my womb was referred to as "a product of conception." The life-giving option of adoption was one I dismissed as too difficult. How could I give my child away? I thought it was easier to snuff out a life. I was a freshman at an Ivy League college, and I had so much to lose. The choice was automatic: have an abortion and forget about it. Get on with life.

At first I was defiant in justifying the decision I had made. It was the late '70s. It was my right to manage my body. Women everywhere told me so. The clump of cells growing inside me was part of *my* body, not a separate and unique life. But in time, the horror of a discarded life started to smolder inside me, burning a hole, a deep abyss of emptiness, inside my heart and soul.

Every June, when the baby that never was, whom I later named Julia, would have been born, I noticed children who would be her age and asked myself a hundred unanswerable questions. What would she have looked like? Would she have had dark hair like me? Would she have dressed in bows and frills, parading around in party shoes, or would she have been a tomboy, swinging upside down from tree branches and clamoring with abandon on the jungle gym? Would she have loved me? I loved her. . . .

The years passed and I buried milestones of her unlived life deep inside me. Off to kindergarten . . . a toothless grin . . . elementary school . . . piano recitals . . . junior high . . . the prom . . . graduation . . . college . . . and perhaps by now married and a mother herself. But I was ashamed . . . so ashamed.

The burden of shame grew heavier and heavier. It was like a rock too heavy to carry. And, oh, how I tried to cast it off! I tried to prevent the secret from consuming me, but denial, justification, shame, guilt, and self-condemnation encased me like a cocoon, holding me captive.

Three years after my abortion I married a wonderful man I met in college, and we settled into a normal life. We started our family right away and had two sons within three years. The following years were busy as my husband completed medical school and I worked with expectant families as a childbirth educator.

When my husband finished his residency training, we decided we wanted another child. I assumed I would get pregnant right away, but we were dealt a hand of secondary infertility and pregnancy loss. My work as a childbirth educator seemed like a cruel joke. I was certain my miscarriage and infertility were punishment from God for the abortion I had.

Five years after embarking on the journey of infertility, we brought home our daughter from Vietnam who shared her birthday with the anniversary of Julia's death. And then, three years later, I found myself pregnant with our youngest daughter.

Choosing Love

Twenty-four years had elapsed since that blustery November day when I had given up my first child. By this time I was a mother of four, and my marriage of twenty-one years was faltering under the pressure of many stresses. Our oldest son, now a sophomore in college, was struggling academically. Our second son was gripped by the seduction of marijuana and in drug rehab. The girls were young and demanding. My life was far from the normalcy I craved.

A storm of chaos raged in my life over which I felt I had no control. I had nowhere to look but toward the heavens. I collapsed into the arms of a loving and patient God who had been calling my name for years. This direction, or choice, had always been available, yet it was not until faced with what appeared to be a dead end that I considered making a U-turn toward a God who had always loved me.

I heard God's voice when I was invited to a local pregnancy care center. It was there I learned more about the healing work offered for people like me suffering from post-abortive stress syndrome. I knew the anguish I felt was real. I just didn't know it was a recognized disorder. I never expected a Christian organization would respond to my pain with love and support. Because of their loving spirit, I learned about a merciful and gracious God who had abounding love for me, could heal me, and could also use my experience to provide healing and comfort to others. It was then I realized God had forgiven me, and cast away my transgressions, *"as far as the east is from the west . . ."* (Psalm 103:12).

In my heart I knew God had forgiven me, but a battle continued to rage inside me: could I forgive myself? I grappled with the feeling of somehow betraying Julia's memory if I forgave myself. I struggled with the difference between forgiving and forgetting. I knew I would never forget, but I also knew I had to forgive myself and discard the cloak of shame I had worn for so many years in order for God to use me to help others.

God has shown me in a real way He has forgiven me. He gave me a daughter, born to another woman in a country halfway around the world on the same November date when so many years before I had made an unforgettable yet forgivable decision. God also ensured Julia's memory in the heart of her father. I found out he also has a daughter born on that same November date. And I have a peace that someday I will be able to see my Julia for the first time and ask for her forgiveness.

For many years I couldn't understand the purpose of my experiences: crisis pregnancy, pregnancy loss, and becoming an adoptive mother. But these experiences have helped shape me into who I am today and have allowed me to see the evidences of God's grace and forgiveness through the intersection of one date and three unique, yet connected, children's lives. I have grieved and let go of the shame. And for this I am grateful for a forgiving and merciful God.

Watching Over You

by Linda Ferris

LINCOLN PARK, MICHIGAN

I was raising my thirteen-year-old son, Michael, alone. I had divorced Michael's father eleven years before. For all those years I was actively involved in everything Michael did. I was always very careful about where he went and who would be there.

One evening I took him and his friend Joe to ski at the nearby ski hill in Riverview, Michigan. It was a nice community ski facility, with an area for food and drinks in the upper loft. I told the boys I would be watching them ski for a while (even though in the evening with the lights on the hill, you could rarely tell any of them apart as they came skiing down). Most parents dropped their kids off and would come back hours later, but before I would feel comfortable about leaving, I had to be sure they were safe and having a good time.

Hour after hour I stood there watching each little figure go up in the ski lift and then slowly ski downward. A couple of times the boys came in for some food and hot chocolate. They laughed and shared their triumphs and defeat of the hill, got warmed up, and off they went again.

After nearly four hours had gone by, I found myself standing in the window feeling a bit lonely, starting to feel sorry for myself, feeling tired and weepy. Thoughts started creeping into my head of how my ex-husband was probably out having a great time, with no responsibilities to tie him down. How great it would be to just be able to go clothes shopping or have some fun, something just for *me* for a change.

Suddenly a voice broke through my self-pitying mood. A young gentleman, whom I had never met, said, "Hi, excuse me . . . but I noticed you've been standing there for hours watching your kids ski, is that right?"

I responded, rather taken aback, "Yes, I have."

He replied, "Well, I just wanted to tell you that if there were more parents in the world like you, this would be a better place." And then he pushed the door open and left as suddenly as he had come.

My mood lifted and a smile came over my face. I had always quoted a passage from the Bible: "Do not forget to entertain strangers, for by so doing some people have entertained angels without knowing it" (Hebrews 13:2). At the moment he spoke I got a very strange but comfortable feeling. Even though I was not aware of the man watching me, he had been aware of my actions. I felt God had sent this man, this angel, to remind me of what was really important in life.

I knew in my heart there was nothing else I'd rather be doing at that moment, and no where else I'd choose to be.

Choosing Love

My Family's Hands

by Sharon Fink

CENTRAL POINT, OREGON

Lyndsay, my beautiful granddaughter, is small for her six years. She has big blue eyes, long eyelashes, and soft curly dark hair. She has been the recipient of more prayers than most humans will ever receive. Her delicate hands have never been able to reach out to receive the wonders of this world. They lie curled up in her little bed. She has cerebral palsy. She doesn't get to eat hot dogs or ice-cream cones. Her mom feeds her through a tube in her tummy. God knew she would need lots of special love, more than most children, so He chose her birthday carefully . . . Valentine's Day.

Like Lyndsay, my father's hands are now closed, too. He's ninety. Only painful massages can unlock the hands that gave openly in ministry to his Lord for so many years. Alzheimer's disease has cruelly closed his hands and his mind, but tears in his eyes and lips puckered to kiss, tell me his heart is still open. He taught my hands how to write and type on the old manual typewriter. I can still see his fingers curled just right on the middle row of keys. He didn't show me the "hunt and peck" method, but the right way to move my fingers two rows up and one row down from the home row *asdfghjkl.*

As I type this story, I look down at my hands and see my pinky finger curling just like his used to. I have the same kind of bumps on my knuckles he has.

My mother, close by in another section of the same nursing home where Dad resides, has a hand closed due to a stroke. It hurts her now to unlock those fingers. Those are the same nimble fingers that played the piano, combed my hair, and wiped my tears when I cried. Now I wipe her tears and stroke her crippled hand. She doesn't know my name anymore, but she always has a smile for me.

I could choose to clench both fists and shake them at God in anger, asking Him why this happened to such dear, undeserving family members. Lyndsay is an innocent child with her whole life before her. Dad and Mom have blessed and been blessed by so many, they don't deserve this kind of sunset years.

But God has used my loved ones as His instruments to unclench my own selfish fists. Their crippled hands have sent me running to my Father, my only source of hope. As I massage their hands, my hands begin to open wider to receive whatever God wants to give me, to thank Him for their lives, and hug those who can't hug back. I choose, daily, to place my open hands into God's nail-scarred hands to receive whatever He wants to place there. It's not always easy, but I remember the wise words of Corrie ten Boom, a survivor of the Holocaust: "When we close our hands, we miss the many blessings God wants to place in them."

Choosing Love

First You Ask *Why?*

by Pamela D. Hallal

INDIANAPOLIS, INDIANA

The day was a glimpse of the arrival of spring. It was not yet warm enough to shed jackets, since winter was refusing to give up chilling the air. Another typical day packed full of meetings, activities, and a long to-do list. One of the tasks was to finish purchasing care package items for our oldest son, Deryk, a Marine deployed to Iraq just forty-eight days ago.

I had been missing him so desperately a week earlier. I recall my husband asking me why I was so teary-eyed and melancholy.

I replied, "I miss Deryk so much! I just need to hear his voice or get a letter from him soon."

God knows the burdens of our hearts. Before the clock struck midnight, the phone rang. I looked up at the clock as I answered it.

"Mom?" said the voice on the other end.

"Deryk!" I exclaimed with a jubilant cry. While intently listening to the wonderful pitch of my son's voice, my heart was singing praises to our Lord. Only He could calm my soul by bringing me such peace, through the happy-go-lucky attitude of my son, in a battlefield thousands of miles away!

But just one week later, standing at my front door, were two Marines in their dress blues, delivering the most dreaded and devastating news two parents can ever hear. I asked God, "Why are they here? Why are they telling me these awful lies? If it's true, why would God ignore my prayers and take my son away?" Silently, tears began flowing; my heart ached to the deepest pit of my soul. My mind reeled, begging and appealing to God. Surely He had not disregarded our prayers. It had to be a mistake!

As the uncontrollable tears poured from my eyes, I clung to the words of my Father in heaven, who protected me from drowning in the sorrow filling my heart.

He brought to mind the verse of the hope of the resurrection: "Brothers, we do not want you to be ignorant about those who fall asleep, or to grieve like the rest of men, who have no hope. We believe that Jesus died and rose again and so we believe that God will bring with Jesus those who have fallen asleep in him" (1 Thessalonians 4:13–14).

My husband and I had two choices facing us. We could choose to disregard everything both we and our beloved son believed about the hope of eternity. We could become angry, bitter, and full of self-pity, making room for Satan to enter. Or we could choose to remain faithful, clinging to Jesus Christ, who bears all pain, relieves all pain, and with an everlasting salve, heals all wounds. For us there was only one choice we could make. God is our refuge and our Rock of strength. We made the decision to honor our son by glorifying God in the ordained life Deryk was chosen to live.

God has been, and continues to be, faithful. It is so much more than just the hope that we will see Deryk again. Hope is not a strong enough emotion alone to accomplish what it is we want. Hope, hand-in-hand with faith, gives us the confidence we need. When we walk in the will of God, we receive what His Word promises. Hebrews 11:1 says, "Now faith is being sure of what we hope for and certain of what we do not see."

Because we have faith in the assurance of things hoped for, and we know Deryk had the same faith, we can endure each day of grieving, while longing for the things not seen.

Accepting the trinity of faith, hope, and love is what moves us through each day; and in the very end, will also move us to the pearly gates of heaven as promised to all who believe and accept Jesus Christ. Hebrews 10:35–36 supplies us the hope in which we cling: "So do not throw away your confidence; it will be richly rewarded. You need to persevere so that when you have done the will of God, you will receive what he has promised."

First I asked why and cried. I then realized I could be thankful and praise God. He gave me two sons: His Son to pay for my spiritual freedom, and my son to free an oppressed people from an evil dictator. I will continue to cling to the Lord. He has been my hope and confidence since my youth, proclaiming His mighty deeds and His unwavering faithfulness. He is the only choice we can make to see us through.

A Homeless Heart

by Renee Willa Hixson

SURREY, BRITISH COLUMBIA, CANADA

It was hot. Sweat glued my thin, sleeveless shirt to the fabric of the driver's seat. The heat radiated off the pavement like a blowtorch. My son Russell sat beside me in the passenger seat. Limp from the summer heat, he stared out the van window lethargically.

I stared straight ahead and drove toward the intersection in front of me. The light quickly turned yellow and then red.

"Oh, great!" I muttered as I put on the brakes. "At this rate we'll never get home."

At least ten traffic lights still separated us from Highway 1, our link to the suburbs. Once we reached it we would have to fight for space with the rest of the minivans deserting the city.

The wait was frustrating. I was a busy pastor's wife and a busy mother. Between errands, housekeeping, and church obligations, there was no time to sit in traffic making sweat stains on my blouse. The futility of my situation made me want to scream.

"Roll up your window!" I snapped to Russell.

"Aw, Mom." Russell interrupted any primal outburst lurking in my throat. He waved his hand slowly out the window hoping to catch a slight breeze. "I gotta have fresh air. It's so hot!"

"I have air-conditioning," I replied tersely. The air-conditioning was not enough in this heat. But there were worse circumstances than no air-conditioning: Main and Terminal. I dreaded this intersection. The two streets crossed between a large McDonald's and a mass transit station known as Main Street Station. Worn brick buildings called "Hotels" offered rooms by the month. It was a haven for the homeless. More than one grocery cart rattled down the sidewalks with someone's entire collection of worldly goods.

The window washers were my worry. They waved their window-cleaning squeegees and ruled the road. Get through the light without paying for a window clean? The odds were against you. If the light changed before your car made it through, you had only one option: Stare straight ahead and ignore the eager eyes of the window washers. It was no wonder the windows of every car were rolled up—with or without air-conditioning. Every car was an island. Every man was for himself.

The light turned yellow just as we stopped. We sat four cars from the light. The panhandlers descended upon the street. Dressed in their uniforms of dingy browns, blacks, and ragged green, they waved their squeegees. Going from car window to car window, the cleaners offered their services.

Thoughts of squeegee rage filled my mind as I glanced around for loose change. I'd heard of one guy who refused to have his window washed. The window washer just reached in and grabbed the guy's wallet. Maybe it really happened. Maybe it didn't. No matter. I was intimidated. A few swear words or an angry scowl would break me. Like other drivers, I'd slowly open the window a crack and push out one or two dollars. It was like some ancient ritual gone urban. We all had to give an offering to "soothe the savage beast."

My head was still shaking in dismay when I noticed no one had approached our car. All the squeegee workers busily squirted and cleaned the car windows ahead. There was no time for them to make it to our car before the light changed. I sighed and leaned back in my seat.

That's when I saw her. A frail ninety pounds of tired flesh. She wobbled closer on impossibly thin jean-clad legs. Her face was dingy and lined with the hopelessness of living on the street. Dark, greasy hair clung to her scalp.

Before I had a chance to move she was at my son's window. I stared. She smiled. Rotten teeth were produced within a frame of dry, chapped lips.

"I'm really hungry," she said lisped through broken teeth. "Can you spare some change?"

"I—just . . . a minute," I dug through my purse. I was a Christian after all. Besides, the money would make her go away quicker. She smelled like a thousand sweaty nights even though she was dressed in a heavy coat. There wasn't too much to spare after our trip to McDonald's. In fact, all I could grope was wads of receipts and a few pens and pencils. Russell poked his finger through the change drawer on the van console. He handed me three pennies and a nickel.

"Eight cents?" I offered fearfully.

She smiled. Several decaying teeth exposed themselves to the sunshine.

"No way, I can't take your last bit of change," she replied warmly. "Keep it."

Keep it? I stared at the emaciated bit of humanity.

"Do you have a little girl at home?" she asked conversationally as she pulled her dirty black bomber jacket closer to her thin frame.

"Well, ah . . . yeah," I replied, not sure why I was disclosing such

Choosing Love

personal information to a total stranger. But, it was true. I did have a little girl at home. My mom was baby-sitting her at that very moment.

The tattered woman reached into her pocket. She pulled out a little purple figure with fuzzy yellow hair.

"I've got something for her. I do. Found this McDonald's toy in the gutter by the restaurant. Been savin' it for the right person. Your little girl might like it. You can give it to her when you get home."

The lady carefully held up her stained and worn offering. I held out an open palm. She gently placed the small figure in my hand. Then the tired little lady smiled again and stepped away from the van.

"God . . . bless . . . you," I stuttered, trying to somehow match offering to offering with a couple of trembling words. But it was too late. She was walking away.

The light turned green. The car behind me honked. I reluctantly glanced in my rearview mirror before I pressed on the gas. The lady in the bomber jacket continued walking down the line of cars. I watched her step up onto the busy sidewalk and disappear among her fellow street dwellers.

"Mom," said Russell as we finally entered the intersection. "What was that all about?"

What else could I say? I was the one driving home to my secure life in the suburbs. She was the one who lived on the streets. I was the one who was very, very busy doing "good deeds" and ministry tasks. God had used her to reach through the layers of my life. My hectic schedule. My busy suburban life. This homeless woman showed what really mattered: sacrificial love—a lesson I needed to learn that day, and one I've remembered for years.

A Wreath and a Cup of Tea

by Margaret Lang

LAS FLORES, CALIFORNIA

Oh, for the things I might have said, the things I might have done.

My eyes were riveted to the inscription beneath the oil painting. Unlike the light and airy impressionist paintings my mom and I had viewed, this masterpiece depicted a somber funeral wreath on a glossy black door. The Monets receded from my memory, but this poignant inscription seared its way into my consciousness.

What finality!

On the subway ride home from the Art Institute of Chicago, I thought about Mom. How close she sat beside me, yet how distant. There were many things I could have said to her or done for her through the years, but I didn't. I did them with Dad instead.

Now that I'm in college, I wonder if it's too late to turn things around.

Like framed pictures from the museum, vignettes of my past appeared before my eyes. I saw Mom seated quietly at the table after another of her delicious home-cooked dinners, while I giggled on Dad's lap.

I saw Dad and I seated on opposite sides of the coffee table focused on a jigsaw puzzle while Mom labored alone over dishes in the kitchen.

As I grew older, I remembered how Dad and I, each with our long strides, power-walked down the street, while Mom, with her shorter legs, lagged farther and farther behind.

At a party, I recalled my gregarious dad and I arm-in-arm, while

Choosing Love

my quieter mom was, well, who knows where? Could she have been lonely in that festive crowd?

The subway jolted to a stop, and with it my former ways. *From now on, it's going to be different.* I want Mom to see how much she means to me. I stole a glance at her seated beside me, prim in her suit and hat, her mind somewhere else.

"What are you thinking, Mom?"

"Oh, just about the troubled girls at my school."

Mom was a devoted teacher, and I knew she helped disadvantaged children in a number of ways. But I hadn't realized before now how deeply she felt for these children.

I wondered if I really knew her. Perhaps I only knew about her. *Love one another as I have loved you* I remembered from the book of John.

That night I gave Mom the hug usually reserved for Dad. She stood stiff like an awkward child who didn't know how to respond.

What can I do to reach her with my love? I asked the Lord, later in bed.

In a flash it occurred to me. Her British heritage was the key. After all, she liked everything English. Maybe I could try to adapt my tomboy persona to meet her more ladylike preferences.

"Mom, could we have a cup of English tea together this afternoon?" I asked the next day, dressed in a skirt.

Startled, she replied, "Why, yes . . . of course, dear."

I noticed how carefully she laid out her best china with silver teapot, pitcher of cream, and bowl of sugar, even with a plate of Scottish shortbread—my favorite. She set the tea service on the low table and poured the tea she had brought back from England. Cups and saucers held rigid, we talked about her recent trip to Cornwall to search out her relatives. Our fingers relaxed their grip as our hearts began to open up.

The next day we repeated the tea party, and the days after that, always at three-o'clock sharp. No matter how busy, we took time out for our pot of English tea.

Formal talk became easy chatter. Mom gave it a name, "girlie gab," and giggled like a schoolgirl when Dad came around to see what we were up to. She even unlocked the longings and secrets of her heart. Each day the intricate threads of our lives wove themselves tighter in a meaningful relationship.

That summer we got so that we preferred each other's company. We sat side-by-side in an oil-painting class. We read and discussed the same historic novels, including the one Mom labored to write about the South. And we locked fingers as we potted chrysanthemums, anticipating the coming of fall and my return to college.

Later, and for many years, my marriage took me miles away from her . . . that is, until the autumn of her life. Dad had passed on, and she suffered a mild stroke. So I brought her back East with me.

That was the summer to delight her with the laughter of children and the playfulness of puppies. It became the fall to shuffle through leaves, feed the ducks, and picnic by the pond. It turned into the winter to snuggle by the fire, carol at the piano, and peruse family photos. It broke into the spring to sniff country lilacs, hear the mockingbird's song and, most important, to sip a cup of English tea together.

Then it was over.

My brother wanted her with him, and I steeled myself for the looming finality of her return to the Midwest. The book of "the things I might have said and the things I might have done" was closing. There was nothing more I could do.

"Good-bye, precious Mom," I said at the airport, through tears. Her soft and radiant smile of thanks was all I needed.

Another summer came and went before I laid a wreath at her gravesite. How transformed it was from the cold wreath in the Art Institute painting. This one was personal, woven intricately with bright memories. I was thankful to have heeded the plea of the heavenly Artist "to love" before the hour had passed. That choice made all the difference in the world.

allison's concluding thoughts

Dear Reader, I can't leave without asking the most important question: Do you have a personal relationship with the eternal God? I'm not talking about "getting a religion." I'm talking about "getting a relationship." You may have read every word of this book and yet never experienced the peace, strength, and hope our authors have shared with you here.

I spent decades of my life looking for fulfillment in all the wrong places. Today I have peace, strength, and hope because there was a time in my life when I accepted Jesus as my personal Savior. This is what I mean by getting a "relationship," not a "religion."

The way is simple: It only takes three steps.

1. Admit you are a sinner: "For all have sinned and fall short of the glory of God" (Romans 3:23).

2. Believe Jesus is God the Son and He paid the wages of your sin: "For the wages of sin is death [eternal separation from God]; but the gift of God is eternal life in Christ Jesus our Lord" (Romans 6:23).

3. Call upon God: "If thou shalt confess with thy mouth the Lord Jesus, and shalt believe in thine heart that God hath raised him from the dead, thou shalt be saved" (Romans 10:9 KJV).

Our Web site has a "Statement of Faith" page you might find interesting and comforting. On that page you will find helpful (and hopeful) links to other spiritually uplifting Web pages. Please visit us at *www.godallowsuturns.com*.

Salvation is a very personal thing. It is between you and God. I cannot have faith enough for you; no one can. The choice is yours alone. Please know this wonderful gift of hope and healing is available to you. You need only reach out and ask for it. It is never too late to make a U-turn toward God . . . no matter where you have been or what you have done. Remember: The choices we make change the story of our life. Please know I am praying for you.

God's Peace and Protection Always,
Allison Bottke

about God Allows U-Turns

Along with these exciting new books published by Bethany House Publishers, we want to share with readers the entire scope of the powerful God Allows U-Turns message of hope and healing.

The broad outreach of this organization includes the book you now hold in your hands, as well as other nonfiction and fiction books for adults, youth, and children. Written by Allison Bottke along with other collaborating authors and co-editors, there are currently seventeen books available under the God Allows U-Turns umbrella brand, with additional books releasing soon, including Allison's first novel in the "chick-lit" genre, *A Stitch in Time,* from Bethany House.

Along with books, the God Allows U-Turns outreach also includes tracts, logo merchandise, a line of greeting cards, a speaking ministry, a foundation, and a daily blog. More than fifty thousand copies of the God Allows U-Turns tract, featuring Allison's powerful testimony of making a U-turn toward God, have been distributed around the world. God Allows U-Turns anthologies have been translated into Japanese and Portuguese.

Sharing the life-saving message that you can never be so lost or so broken that you can't turn toward God is Allison's main passion in her life and in her ministry.

Visit your local bookstore or the God Allows U-Turns Web site to find out more about this exciting ministry that is helping to change lives: *www.godallowsuturns.com* or write:

> Allison Bottke
> God Allows U-Turns
> PO Box 717
> Faribault, MN 55021–0717
> editor@godallowsuturns.com

future volumes of
God Allows U-Turns

The stories you have read in this volume were submitted by readers just like you. From the very start of this inspiring book series, it has been our goal to encourage people from around the world to submit their slice-of-life true short stories for publication.

God Allows U-Turns stories must touch the emotions and stir the heart. We are asking for well-written, personal inspirational pieces showing how faith in God can inspire, encourage, heal, and give hope. We are looking for human-interest stories with a spiritual application, affirming ways in which Christian faith is expressed in the everyday choices of life. We understand that the choices we make change the story of our life.

Our prayer is to publish additional volumes in the U-Turns series every year. Your true story can be from 300 to 1,500 words and must be told with drama, description, and dialogue. Our writer's guidelines are featured on our Web site, and we encourage you to read them carefully. We apologize, but due to the huge response to our request for true stories, we can no longer accept snail-mail submissions. All submissions must be via e-mail or our Web site. Please be advised we cannot respond in any way to the stories submitted. If you wish to know if they have been received, request a "read receipt" at the time of submission. You will only be contacted in the event your story is selected for possible inclusion in a specific volume we are working on.

Fees are paid for stories we publish, and we will be sure to credit you for your submission. Remember, our Web site is filled with up-to-date information about the book project. Additionally, you might want to take advantage of signing up to be on our free ezine list for Internet users. For a list of current *God Allows U-Turns* books open to submissions, as well as related opportunities, visit us at *www.godallowsuturns.com.*

sharing the success:
the God Allows U-Turns foundation

One of the most profound lessons in the Bible is giving. The Holy Bible is quite clear in teaching us how we are to live our lives. Scripture refers to this often, and never has the need to share with others been so great.

> Give, and it will be given to you. A good measure, pressed down, shaken together and running over, will be poured into your lap. For with the measure you use, it will be measured to you. (Luke 6:38)

In keeping with the lessons taught us by the Lord our God, we are pleased to have the opportunity to donate a portion of the net profits of every *God Allows U-Turns* book to one or more nonprofit Christian charity. These donations are made through the God

Allows U-Turns Foundation, a funding mechanism established by Kevin and Allison Bottke as a way to share the success of the growing U-Turns outreach ministry.

Additionally, the Strength of Choice Award is also a significant aspect of this vision. Established in 2002, the God Allows U-Turns Strength of Choice Award is given annually at the Golden Scroll Awards banquet sponsored by AWSA—the Advanced Writers and Speakers Association, held just prior to the opening of CBA International.

The God Allows U-Turns Strength of Choice Award goes to the person who in the previous year best exemplified a consistent determination to rise above difficult circumstances while maintaining a clear focus on the One who not only "allows" U-turns, but who remains with us on any life journey, no matter how many twists and turns it may bring. The recipient of this award outwardly lives Philippians 4:12–13: "I know what it is to be in need, and I know what it is to have plenty. I have learned the secret of being content in any and every situation, whether well fed or hungry, whether living in plenty or in want. I can do everything through him who gives me strength." Past recipients have been Gene and Carol Kent, Ramona Richards, and Dan Penwell.

For more details visit the Web site at: *www.godallowsuturns.com.*

about the authors

ALLISON BOTTKE lives in southern Minnesota on a twenty-five-acre hobby farm with her entrepreneur-husband, Kevin. She is a relatively "new" Christian, coming to the fold in 1989 as a result of a dramatic life U-turn. The driving force behind God Allows U-Turns, she has a growing passion to share with others the healing and hope offered by the Lord Jesus Christ. Allison has a wonderful ability to inspire and encourage audiences with her down-to-earth speaking style as she relates her personal testimony of how God orchestrated a dramatic U-turn in her life. Lovingly dubbed "The U-Turns Poster Girl," you can find out more about Allison by visiting her information page on the book's Web site: *www.godallowsuturns.com/aboutauthor.htm.*

CHERYLL HUTCHINGS has been a Christian since the age of twelve and has always let God lead her in life. The best adventure He's led her on so far has been joining the God Allows U-Turns project on the ground floor of the ministry when it began in 2000. Married to Bob for twenty-eight years, they have a twenty-three-year-old son named Aaron, who is working full time in the computer industry, and a twenty-year-old son named Scott, who is a corporal in the United States Marine Corps. They live in the country in a rambling ranch in Medina, Ohio, which sits on several acres of peaceful seclusion, surrounded by the Lord's beautiful nature and wildlife.

about our internet web site

We first announced God Allows U-Turns on the World Wide Web in February of 2000. The Lord used this avenue of communication to reach across all borders: geographic as well as racial, political, denominational, and social. Stories began to come to us via our Web site, first by the dozens, then hundreds, and now thousands.

While our Web site is specific to the God Allows U-Turns book series, you will find we also offer important links to other major Christian Web sites, links we encourage you to visit. Additionally, we have placed a "Statement of Faith" page on our site to clearly establish our beliefs. Also of note is the page "How to Be Born Again" (*www.godallowsuturns.com/stmtfaith.htm*). This section on our Web site is visited by thousands of people every year.

The global opportunities a Web site provides are mind-boggling, but we need your help to make the kind of impact we know is possible. Please visit our Web site and forward it to your family and friends. Virtually everyone has a story to tell, and future volumes will enable those stories to be told. We are accepting true short stories now for future volumes. Visit our "Future Volumes" page on our Web site to find out more.

Remember, our Web site is filled with up-to-date information about the book project. You will be able to access tour and book-signing calendars on the site, as well as read stories from the current volume. Additionally, you might want to take advantage of signing up for our free ezine list for Internet users. Don't miss out on current news and reviews. We invite you to visit our daily blog at *www.godallowsuturns.blogspot.com.*

about our contributors

Nancy C. Anderson (*www.NancyCAnderson.com*) is the award-winning author of *Avoiding the Greener Grass Syndrome: How to Grow Affair-Proof Hedges Around Your Marriage*. She is also a popular speaker for women's and couples' events. Nancy lives in California with her husband of twenty-seven years and their teenage son.

Esther M. Bailey is a freelance writer living in Scottsdale, Arizona. Besides more than one thousand published credits, she is the author of three books. In her leisure time she most enjoys dining out with friends. E-mail her at baileywick@juno.com or visit *www.baileywick.net*.

Nancy Baker resides in College Station, Texas, with her husband. Upon retirement, she pursued her lifelong love of writing and has been published in national magazines and numerous anthologies. She directs the ministry to the sick program at her church and is a hospice volunteer. E-mail her at nanbaker@cox-internet.com.

Pat Toornman Bales still lives on a small farm just south of Brighton, Colorado, where she enjoys keeping a few sheep and chickens (with miscellaneous other critters) and knowing God will show "His purpose" for her life when it's the right time. E-mail her at bales11@netzero.net.

Shelly (Michele) Beach has been published in secular and religious markets in a wide variety of genres. She is a college writing instructor, communications consultant, and public speaker. Her speaking and writing ministry focuses on God's redemption of even our most painful experiences. E-mail her at sandscribbler@charter.net.

Rita Billbe and her husband own a resort, Angels Retreat, on the Arkansas White River. Her publishing credits include: *Chicken Soup for the Sister's Soul, Chicken Soup for Every Mom's Soul, Lightnin' Ridge Journal, Wee Ones* magazine, and *Journal of the American Donkey and Mule Society*. Visit her Web site at *www.whiteriver.net/angels-retreat/* or e-mail angelret@flippinweb.com.

Debbye Butler's work appears in print and online publications, including *Indiana Christian News* and *The Indianapolis Star*. Her passion project is to complete her book for primary caregivers of terminally ill parents. Debbye served that role for her mother, to whom the book will be dedicated. E-mail her at dbutlerabc@sbcglobal.net

Connie Sturm Cameron is married to Chuck, and they have two children, Chase and Chelsea. Connie is a freelance writer, and this story is excerpted from her book *God's Gentle Nudges*. Contact her at *www.conniecameron.com* or e-mail conniec@ netpluscom.com.

Janet Carpenter, a successful artist whose oils hang in museums, fine homes, and galleries in several states, was once a home economist. She wrote columns, did radio commentaries, and produced TV programs. Janet married her beloved Robert forty-five years ago. They have seven grandchildren. E-mail her at rdc2620@aol.com.

Elena Chevalier is a friend of God, a wife, and a mother of four. She resides in Benton, New Hampshire, where she enjoys studying God's Word and sharing its wonderful truths with others through writing and speaking. She is a reporter for the local newspaper. E-mail her at nhwriter@gmail.com.

Jennifer Devlin is a retired Army wife and women's ministry leader with a vibrant speaking, writing, and teaching ministry. She is blessed with a wonderful husband and son, and they reside in northern Alabama. Please visit her Web site at *www. ministryforlife.com* or e-mail her at jennifer@ministryforlife .com for more details.

Jan Eckles is an inspirational speaker, writer, and author of *Trials of Today, Treasures for Tomorrow: Overcoming Adversities in Life*. Need some inspiration? Visit Jan at *www.janeckles.com* or e-mail her at jekles@cfl.rr.com.

Kriss Erickson is a versatile freelance writer who has had over three hundred items published since she began writing professionally in 1981. She has often illustrated her work, and has provided photographs when needed. Visit Kriss's Web site at: *http://slverkriss.tripod.com*, or e-mail her at slverkriss@aol.com.

Anita Estes (Jeannette Light) resides in the Hudson Valley and is an art treacher, painter, freelance writer, and book club leader. She is listed in Who's Who of American Teachers for 2000 and 2005. Her writing appears in several different publications, and she is the author of *When God Speaks*. E-mail her at anitawriter7 @yahoo.com or visit *www.anitaestes.com*.

Eva Marie Everson has made an impact in Christian publishing in a matter of a few years by crossing genres and rarely being predictable. Since 1999 she has written, compiled, and edited books of both fiction and nonfiction, including *The Potluck Club* and *Sex, Lies, and the Media*. Visit her Web site at *www.evamarie everson.com*.

Phyllis Farringer's work has appeared in various publications, including *Decision, Women Alive!* and *Focus on Your Child*. She serves on the Advisory Board for Heart of America Christian Writers' Network. She and her husband, Doug, live in Olathe, Kansas.

Sharon L. Fawcett is a freelance writer and speaker with a passion to spread hope. Her favorite pursuit is adventuring with God. With their two daughters, Sharon and husband, Tim, reside in a rural community in eastern Canada, between the forest and the sea. Visit her at *www.sharonfawcett.com*.

Linda Ferris is a registered nurse practicing in southeast Michigan. She enjoys praising God, writing, quilting, and spending time with friends and family. Her son Michael is now married and he and Carrie just moved into their first home. Linda can be reached at *LAFRN10@aol.com*.

Sharon Fink is a retired university career counselor with a degree in communications and a creative writing minor. She does freelance writing while traveling around the United States with her husband. She is a committed Christian and member of Oregon Christian Writers. E-mail her at fink@sou.edu.

Sue Foster is a published author of short stories and articles. She serves as a Ministering Elder at Capistrano Community Church. Sue and her husband, Steve, reside in Laguna Niguel, California. They are the parents of two grown daughters.

Tammy Gehman ministers to those who feel worn out, defeated, or stuck in their past. With refreshing honesty and bold confidence, she gives evidence that "God can do anything—far more than you can ever imagine." She can be reached at *www.tammy gehman.com*.

Carol Genengels' stories have appeared in *Reminisce, Stories for the Spirit-Filled Believer, God Allows U-Turns, Chicken Soup for the Soul, God Answers Mom's Prayers,* and *Journeys of Friendship.* Her book, *Unfailing Love,* details Carol's life story. E-mail her at awtcarolg@aol.com.

Nancy B. Gibbs is a pastor's wife, author of four books, and motivational speaker. Nancy writes two weekly newspaper columns and has contributed to numerous magazines, devotional guides, and anthologies. Nancy may be reached by e-mail at Daiseydood@aol.com or through her Web site at *www.nancybgibbs.com*.

Anne Goodrich is a graphic designer for an educational service agency in Kalamazoo, Michigan, as well as owner of her own design business. Her faith is her first passion, but other loves include her children, family, friends, church, autumn leaves, and french silk pie. Contact her at *www.goodrichdesign.net.*

Dianna Graveman is a teacher and freelance writer. She has a bachelor's degree in education and an M.F.A. in writing. She lives in St. Charles, Missouri, with her husband, three almost-grown children, and a loveable mutt named Tramp.

Cheryl Haggard is a refreshing author, speaker, and mother to Calvin, Caleb, and Molly, who share a rare pediatric immune disorder. Cheryl is determined to encourage you with the gift of side-splitting laughter. Married fourteen years to football coach Mark, the Haggards hail from Star, Idaho. E-mail her at chaggard04@cableone.net.

Pamela Hallal, husband, and family are small-business owners and reside in Indianapolis. They are longtime members of College Park Church. As a strong military advocate, Pamela frequently speaks publicly, motivating others to support our troops while sharing inspiring truths from God. E-mail her at p.hallal@ integrity.com.

Audrey Kletscher Helbling lives in Faribault, Minnesota, with her husband and three children. She enjoys gardening and photography, but is most passionate about writing. Audrey has been published in *God Answers Prayers—Military Edition, Minnesota Moments, The Lutheran Digest,* poetry anthologies, greeting cards, and elsewhere.

Renee Hixson, born in Michigan and raised in Texas, now resides in beautiful British Colombia with husband, Dennis, and children Nathan, Russell, and Lily. The fourth, Josh, has flown the nest to JBU. Besides missing her firstborn, she is working on a romantic adventure novel. E-mail her at rhixson@telus.net.

Elaine Ingalls Hogg wrote "Remembering Honey" to help children understand grief. She has written a number of inspirational stories and devotionals and a popular history, "When Canada Joined Cape Breton." Elaine speaks at writing workshops and shares her faith with women's groups. Visit her Web site at *http://elainehogg.tripod.com* or e-mail her at authorhogg@yahoo.ca.

Betty J. Johnson, inspirational writer of devotions and articles, lives in Parker, Colorado. She is a contributor to numerous devotional books, facilitates a grief-support group, participates in several Bible studies, and spends fun time with her new husband and their large blended family.

Venice Kichura is a freelance writer who lives in South Windsor, Connecticut, with her husband, Ed. They have two grown sons and four grandchildren who live in Florida. She's written several Christian articles and works as a substitute teacher. E-mail her at vmkichura@cox.net.

Karen Kosman is a wife, mother, grandmother, inspirational speaker, and freelance writer. Karen's joy and zest for life warms hearts. She has authored stories in compilation books and magazine articles. Her latest article, "Innocence Reclaimed," appeared in *Power for Living, 2005*. Contact her at ComKosman@aol.com or *www.renewalofhope.com*.

Margaret Lang received her Bachelor of Arts from Brown University. She teaches women's groups in California. Margaret has stories published in *Chicken Soup for the Soul* and *Christian Miracles*. Her daughter is a physician/missionary, her son a youth pastor, and she has two granddaughters.

Marcia Krugh Leaser has been writing for many years. Her work consists mostly of poetry, but she has written books as well. Married with two grown daughters and five grandchildren, writing is an important part of her life, and she considers it a gift from God.

Jaye Lewis is an award-winning writer and contributing author to *Chicken Soup for the Soul*. Jaye is seeking a publisher for her book, *Entertaining Angels*, which celebrates the miraculous in everyday life. Her Web site is *www.entertainingangels.org*. E-mail Jaye at jayelewis@comcast.net.

Julie Mathiason-Bendel is the mother of three children. She and her husband, Mark, own and operate Heritage House Elder Care in Faribault, Minnesota. As the Director of Nursing, Julie continues to serve the elderly population. E-mail her at hhec@charter.net.

Carol McGalliard is a writer and speaker in Greensboro, North Carolina. Her articles have appeared in numerous publications. She is director of Journey, a ministry for survivors of abuse. "In surprising ways, God has restored what abuse stole from me. How can I keep silent?" Visit her Web site at *http://home .earthlink.net/carolwrite*.

Geri Moran is a writer, entrepreneur, and craft artist living in New York. She likes to make people smile with her writing, products, and business services. Her own happiness comes from being with friends, family, her son, Paul, and from visiting Mystic, Connecticut.

Darla Noble, married twenty-five years to John, and mother of four, owns and operates a family sheep farm and greenhouse. She writes children's ministry skits and personal devotions and is currently working on *Through the Eyes of a Shepherd*, scriptural principles brought to life through caring for the flock.

Maggi Normile has an associate's degree in theater and a B.A. in English with a concentration in film and drama studies from Clarion University of Pennsylvania. In her spare time she enjoys watching movies, reading, and listening to music. She lives in Moon Township, Pennsylvania. E-mail her at mnormile@hotmail.com.

Pamela V. Norton spent eighteen years in the New Age Movement after turning her back on her evangelical faith. In 2001 she returned to Jesus and now writes and speaks on the hidden dangers of popular spirituality, mind sciences, and mainstream occult practices. Visit her Web site *www.pvnorton.com* or e-mail her at pvn@pvnorton.com.

Marie Partain is a novice writer whose major accomplishments have been in competitions sponsored by Foothills Writers Guild. "Full Circle" was published in *A Cup of Comfort for Nurses*. Her favorite genres include creative nonfiction and short stories. Contact her at PartainG@aol.com.

Diane H. Pitts serves her community as a physical therapist, but her greatest joy is being wife to Darrell and mother to their three boys. (They'll let her work as long as she promises to cook every now and then.) Visit her Web site at *www.dianehpitts.com*.

Connie Pombo is an inspirational speaker, author, and founder of Women's Mentoring Ministries, a ministry helping local churches create a mentoring ministry and stronger leadership. She and husband, Mark, recently celebrated their thirtieth wedding anniversary. Together they conduct marriage seminars. Visit *www.womenmentoringministries.com* or e-mail her at pom644@earthlink.net.

Cindy Powell is the Director of Women at the Well Ministries and is working on a book tentatively titled *The Well: Stories of Real Women and Their Encounters with a Real God*, intertwining stories of women in Scripture with testimonies of modern-day women. Visit her at *www.watwministries.org*.

Kathy Pride has a passion for encouraging people to take the tatters and loose ends of their lives and weave them into lives of new possibility. She is a wife, mother, author, speaker, and parent educator. Her first book, *Home Invasion: When Drugs Seduce Your Teen*, will be released by AMG in 2006. Please visit her at *www.tapestryministry.com*.

Carolyn Byers Ruch, wife, mother, and friend, writes about tough issues. She is passionate about equipping parents to face twenty-first-century realities, protecting children from sexual abuse, and encouraging survivors toward healing on this side of heaven. E-mail her at undeserveddisgrace@comcast.net.

Tonya Ruiz is a dynamic communicator and Bible teacher who speaks nationally about some of today's most important issues. She is a pastor's wife, homeschooling mother, and grandmother who calls Southern California home. Visit her Web site at *www.TonyaRuiz.com* or e-mail her at Tonya@TonyaRuiz.com.

Margaret Shauers has been a freelance writer for forty years, with publications in many religious and secular magazines. She works with church youth and Crisis Management Team at First

Presbyterian Church in Great Bend, Kansas. E-mail her at mshauers@mac.com.

Susan Skitt is an inspirational writer and speaker whose writing has appeared in a women's devotional book. She enjoys the daily adventure of life in Christ with her husband and two sons. E-mail her at skskitt@comcast.net.

Brenda Sprayue is an Indiana resident, freelance writer, and mother of two. She contributes frequently to *Today's Christian Woman* magazine and is in the self-editing stage of her first inspirational novel. She can be contacted at bsprayue@sbcglobal.net.

Betty Walker was born in Portland, Oregon, and moved to California and attended schools there through UC Berkeley. She married in 1943, was widowed, then remarried in 1963, and widowed ten years later. She was saved in 1937, and is now eighty-six years young.

Sharen Watson currently resides in Highlands Ranch, Colorado. Married twenty-five years to Ray, they have one daughter, a son-in-law, two sons, and one spoiled Lhasa Apso, Gia. Sharen is a speaker, author, and founder of Words for the Journey Christian Writer's Guild. Please visit *www.wordsforthejourney.org* or e-mail her at IRite4Him@aol.com.

Suzannah Willingham is a freelance writer living in South Carolina. Her publishing credits include *The Upper Room* and *Stories for a Teen's Heart, Book 2*. Additionally, she writes on a regular basis for a regional magazine.

Gayle Zinda is a former nurse and business owner, working with cancer, burn, and auto-accident clients to refresh their inner and outer image. A member of Wisconsin National Speaker Association, she lives with husband, Michael, and two sons, Adam and Nick, plus five bonus kids and one grandson, Colin. Visit her Web site at *www.Gayle-Pinklemonade.com.*

Books by Allison Bottke

God Allows U-Turns for Teens
God Allows U-Turns for Women

A Stitch in Time
– a novel –

*I Can't Do It All**

*with Tracie Peterson and Dianne O'Brian